TERRORS AND EXPERTS

TERRORS AND EXPERTS

ADAM PHILLIPS

HARVARD UNIVERSITY PRESS
Cambridge, Massachusetts

First Harvard University Press paperback edition, 1997

Library of Congress Cataloging-in-Publication Data

Phillips, Adam.
Terrors and experts / Adam Phillips.
p.   cm.
Includes bibliographical references and index.
ISBN 0-674-87479-X (cloth)
ISBN 0-674-87480-3 (pbk.)
1. Psychoanalysis.   2. Freud, Sigmund, 1856-1939.
3. Psychoanalytic counseling.   4. Psychoanalysts.
5. Psychotherapist and patient.   I. Title.
BF175.P437   1996
150.19'5—dc20   95-38506

for Mia Rose

Some may perhaps be startled, and cry, 'How comes this sudden change?' To which I answer, 'I am a changeling.' I think that is a full answer.

Andrew Marvell, *The King's Speech*

No reasonable man, I readily agree, would want space travel as such; because he wants to know, in any proposal for travel, whether he would go farther and fare worse. A son of my own at about the age of twelve, keen on space travel like the rest of them, saw the goat having kids and was enough impressed to say, 'It's better than space travel.' It is indeed absolutely or metaphysically better, because it is coming out of the nowhere into here.

William Empson, 'Donne the Space Man'

I do not know how many of you keep a list of the kinds of fool you make of yourselves.

J. L. Austin, *A Plea for Excuses*

Unhuman forms must not assert their roles.

Veronica Forrest-Thomson, 'Not Pastoral Enough'

Contents

Acknowledgements

Different versions of the chapters in this book appeared in the *London Review of Books, Raritan, Psychodynamic Counselling, Island Review* (Tasmania), *The Yearbook of the Belgian Psychoanalytic Society* and *Psychoanalytic Dialogues*. A version of Chapter 6 was published in *The Mind Object*, ed. Corrigan and Gordon (New Jersey, Aronson, 1995).

Once again I am particularly grateful to Mary-Kay Wilmers at the *London Review of Books*, and Dick Poirier and Suzanne Hyman at *Raritan*. These journals, and their editors, have made the kind of things I write possible.

The clinical work that informs the chapters in this book has been sustained by conversations with Alex Coren, Glenda Fredman, Paul van Heeswyk, Morian Roberts and Peter Wilson. Jacqueline Rose made the writing of this book more of a pleasure. Hugh Haughton was, as ever, a necessary reader. Conversations with Lawrence Jacobson, Debbie Waxenberg and John Forrester have contributed more to this book than they may realise.

Preface

Iris Murdoch once suggested that to understand any philosopher's work we must ask ourselves what he or she is frightened of. To understand any psychoanalyst's work – both as a clinician and as a writer – we should ask ourselves what he or she loves: because psychoanalysis is about the unacceptable and about love, two things we may prefer to keep apart, and that Freud found to be inextricable. If there is a way of talking about psychoanalysis as a scandal, without spuriously glamorizing it, then one way of doing it is simply to say that Freud discovered that love was compatible, though often furtively, with all that it was meant to exclude. There are, in other words – and most literature is these other words – no experts on love. And love, whatever else it is, is terror.

In Freud's view our first loves are both forbidding and forbidden. Our parents (or the people who care for us) must protect us from the ordinary catastrophes of childhood – hunger, the cold, the devastations of abandonment – and they must also set limits to our sexual desire for them. By the logic of the Oedipus complex the survivor becomes a lover through frustration. Caught between the harshness of the world and the urgency of his or her instincts, the child is born with a readiness for terror. Psychoanalysis affirms that there is something unmanageable about being a person, and it is this that makes a person who he or she is. The frenzy of a baby, the tantrum or phobia of the older child, the panic of adolescent self-consciousness: the demonic – possession by alien meanings – starts at home. Fear is always familiar.

The child must learn to bear frustration, the adult must learn not to (it has to be that way round). But from a psychoanalytic point of view there is an inevitable complicity between desire and the forbidden, between sexuality and the unattainable. Pleasure is its

xi

own punishment. Psychoanalysis starts with the story that we are too much for ourselves; that we are, in a sense, terrorized by an excess of feeling, by an impossibility of desire. And it is terror, of course, that traditionally drives us into the arms of the experts; that 'Brings the priest and the doctor/In their long coats/Running over the fields', as Philip Larkin writes in his poem 'Days'. Psychoanalysis, like religion and medicine, turns panic into meaning. It makes fear bearable by making it interesting. And it does this in the most ordinary way: through conversation with another person. This, Freud's still new remedy suggests, is what other people are for, to make a difference. Talking changes the way things look. Freud, in other words, never lost sight of a fundamental question: What good are other people? And so, by implication, What does a psychoanalyst have that someone might need, or rather be able to use? Our relationship to experts is a picture of the way we need. What are people doing, what are people up to, when they consult and believe their experts? Or, indeed, when they begin to think of themselves as experts, with all the tangled history of that word? As the OED tells us, 'expert' means both 'tried, proved by experience ... an authority, a specialist', and also 'having no part in ... devoid of, free from'. As Freud showed, such 'antithetical words' do a lot of work for us.

This book addresses the question of what psychoanalysts are experts on (or of) – childhood, sexuality, love, development, dreams, art, the unconscious, unhappiness, how to live and who to be – and what Freud's idea of the unconscious does to the idea of expertise, of being a skilled and competent practitioner of anything, including psychoanalysis itself. With his description of the unconscious and the dream-work, Freud gave the expert – the expert in any field – a new agon and a new collaborator; and, of course, a new source of terror. If we are not, as Freud insisted, masters in our own houses, what kinds of claims can we make for ourselves? In what senses can we know what we are doing? From a psychoanalytic point of view, people are not only the animals who can make promises, but also the animals that can't help breaking them.

If everything now is increasingly subject to expertise – from mourning to making love – with child rearing, in particular, as a growth industry; if we are living in the age of the specialist, then psychoanalysis can be useful as a critique of the whole project of wanting authorities. It can help us sort out what is, in fact, subject to what we call expertise; and, of course, what the alternatives to it may be. (If learning verse-forms and reading poems doesn't make you a poet, then what does? My need for a heart-surgeon is different from my need for a philosopher.) In this book the psychoanalyst is, among other things, a figure for the ironies of expertise – an emblem for the puzzles of competence. There is a useful difference, as psychoanalysis itself can show us, between having a skill – being admirable, or emulatable – and needing to dominate people. A talent is not a weapon in every culture. Unusual ways of doing things only necessitate assertions of superiority to quell doubt.

'A class of experts,' the philosopher John Dewey wrote, 'is inevitably so removed from common interests as to become a class with private knowledge, which in social matters is not knowledge at all.' From a psychoanalytic point of view, there can be no private knowledge, only knowledge that has been hidden (an esoteric psychoanalysis is a contradiction in terms). The psychoanalyst, if he knows anything, knows about the suffering entailed by certain kinds of privacy; indeed, symptoms are forms of private knowledge, expressions of private interests. Psychoanalysis can make both the private social and the anti-social available for comment. And it can make us wonder, by the same token, what we use ideas of privacy to protect ourselves from.

Psychoanalysis, as each of the chapters in this book shows from a different perspective, radically revises our versions of competence, and our notions of a professional self (dreams are very unprofessional). And to analyse a transference, of course, is to analyse a person's need for belief, their craving for experts. We don't celebrate hurdlers when they fall over, or comedians when they aren't funny. And politicians in Western democracies do not get elected on the basis of their capacity for hesitation, or their willingness to sustain contradictory points of view, or their ability to change their minds, or their impassioned support for the opposition's point of view. Psychoanalysis gives us a language to notice this and wonder why it is so. And, by the same token, it puts up for grabs the question of what makes a good analyst. It is part of the mystique of expertise, which Freud both rumbled and cultivated, to believe that because a person has done a recognized or legitimated official training they are then qualified to claim something more than that they have done the training (doing something properly is a way of not doing it differently). Being a member of a club tells you nothing about a person's kindness, or cunning. The transference of psychoanalysts to Freud, to their theory, and to their training institutions, has been stultifying; and it is now, in pre-Freudian terms, beyond a joke (to call it an irony does not do it justice). Psychoanalysts take themselves, and their professionalization, too seriously, something their theory should make them a bit suspicious of. 'In accepting the hat', Owen Chadwick wrote of Cardinal Newman, 'he lost nothing of his unpomp'. The unconscious, for which no one ever receives a hat, should be a continual (secular) reminder of unpomp.

From my point of view a psychoanalyst is anyone who uses what were originally Freud's concepts of transference, the unconscious, and the dream-work in paid conversations with people about how they want to live. The fact that there are psychoanalytic trainings at all, (there were none when psychoanalysis began and was at its most creative), and the ways in which they choose to organize themselves, begs the question of what psychoanalysis is, or rather, is like – medicine, music, friendship, initiation, meteorology, parenting, guessing? And, of course, the question of what it is to learn something. Psychoanalysis can make all these issues more interesting, and more amusing, than they are conventionally allowed to be. A psychoanalyst, for example, has to learn how not to know what he is doing and how to go on doing it.

But psychoanalysis is always at risk of becoming the paradigm of what Wordsworth called, in a famous passage in *The Prelude*, 'Knowledge . . . purchased with the loss of power'; and by power, of course, he did not mean coercion but something more akin to inspiration. As everyone knows, psychoanalysis is very expensive knowledge. By costing so much, in every sense, it sustains its élitism. And élitism, and what used to be called mental health – and should be called living a good life – are mutually exclusive.

The élitism of psychoanalysts – beginning with Freud's aspiration, at least in the early years of his supposedly 'new science', to be allied with the prestigious profession of medicine – was reactive, I think, to an anxiety about assimilation. At first the question was, How did the psychoanalysis that Freud invented fit in with the prevailing contemporary medical specializations? And then a perhaps more daunting question: How would psychoanalysts, fleeing from Nazism, find a place in their newly adopted countries? Could these *émigrés* legitimate themselves when psychoanalysis itself patently revealed the senses in which people were always at odds with their culture? Freud had discovered something that very soon became literally true: that people live under assumed names. For very understandable reasons, it was difficult for the early analysts to resist respectability. And yet it was clear that psychoanalysis, by definition, clashed with the available moral vocabularies. The unconscious, after all, describes that part of ourselves that joins in without ever fitting in.

The language of psychoanalysis, for example, very quickly got (and gets) snarled up with the old-fashioned language of 'will', with which it is incompatible. In relation to the unconscious, you can't try, or make an effort; you can't force yourself to free-associate or aim to make a slip of the tongue, or plan a dream. But muddling these languages turns each version of psychoanalysis into a covert moral injunction: try to be good (Klein); try to be spontaneous (Winnicott); try to be eccentric to yourself (Lacan). If the unconscious is that which does not fit in, why has it been so difficult to sustain non-compliant versions of psychoanalysis? It is bizarre that the splitting of psychoanalytic groups is considered to be a problem: the psychoanalyst, by definition, is someone with an ear for dissenting voices. But the risk is that he becomes someone who can only patronize them. In so far as the psychoanlyst becomes an expert on how people should live – becomes, that is to say, any kind of guru, any kind of official or unofficial expert – he has complied. The psychoanalyst is a professional who sustains his competence by resisting his own authority. The unconscious, at least as Freud described it, is another word for the death of the guru.

If psychoanalysis cannot tell people how to live, it *should* still be able to make people feel better, but often in unexpected ways (only the patient is in a position to detect an improvement). It should, in other words, be that most unlikely thing: an interesting hedonism. But it is only just beginning to get the kind of public scrutiny, the intelligent hostility, it needs, and that will allow people to decide – both the people who can afford it and the people who can't – whether it's worth keeping. No one needs psychoanalysis but some people might want it. Psychoanalysis, as theory and practice, should not pretend to be important instead of keeping itself interesting (importance is a cure for nothing). You would think, reading the professional literature, that it was psychoanalysis that mattered and not what it was about. It is not the future of psychoanalysis that anyone should be concerned about, but rather the finding of languages for what matters most to us; for what we suffer from and for, for how and why we take our pleasures. Sometimes, for some people, psychoanalysis can be one of these languages. Fortunately, there are plenty of others; no one language has a monopoly on our ignorance.

Psychoanalysis, as this book tries to show, teaches us the meaning – the sublimity – of our ignorance; it teaches us that we don't often know what we are saying (which is another way of describing the demonic: my word is my bond despite me, I always say more than I have agreed to). No amount of scientific research will diminish the waywardness of our words; there will always be the clamour of the incongruous. And psychoanalysts are well placed to take a strong stand against the enemies of ambiguity. But when psychoanalysts spend too much time with each other, they start believing in psychoanalysis. They begin to talk knowingly, like members of a religious cult. It is as if they have understood something. They forget, in other words, that they are only telling stories about stories; and that all stories are subject to an unknowable multiplicity of interpretations. The map becomes the ground beneath their feet;

and maps are always a smaller ground. Psychoanalysts need to be attentive to the fascination of fictions, and the morals of words. But they are always tempted to become the experts on the canon of plausible interpretations, of what should be said when. Giving the unconscious elocution lessons is unpromising. In so far as psychoanalysis merely traffics in new proprieties, in fresh forms of respectability, it betrays something of its radical legacy as a conversation in which people cannot help but experiment with themselves. When psychoanalysis loses its unusual capacity to both comfort and unsettle – and its modern sense that you can't have one without the other – it becomes either a form of compulsory radicalism or a new way to learn an old obedience. It was, after all, to the subtleties of compliance that Freud addressed himself. If psychoanalysis is not the means to a personal style, it merely hypnotizes people with a vocabulary.

The psychoanalyst and her so-called patient share a project. The psychoanalyst, that is to say, must ask herself not, Am I being a good analyst (am I wild enough, am I orthodox enough, have I said the right thing)? But, What kind of person do I want to be? There are plenty of people who will answer the first question for her. Faced with the second question, there may be terrors but there are no experts.

Terrors and Experts: An Introduction

I

After all, one can only say something if one has learned to talk.
Wittgenstein, *Philosophical Investigations*

Children unavoidably treat their parents as though they were experts on life. They, and other adults, are the people from whom the child learns what is necessary. But children make demands on adults which the adults don't know what to do with. It is, for example, clear to everyone concerned that adults are unable to answer, in any satisfactory way, several of the child's questions. The so-called facts of life are hardly a convincing answer – for anybody – to why people have sex, or where babies come from. Often, from the child's point of view, answers merely interrupt questions. Whether children are amusing, or irritating, or endearing, or even 'little philosophers', once they learn to talk they create, and suffer, a certain unease about what they can do with words. Paradoxically, it is the adult's own currency – words – that reveals to them the limits of adult authority. The adults are not fully competent with their own instruments, but there is nobody else for the child to appeal to. Children go on asking, of course, but eventually they have to settle for the adult's exhausted impatience, and the fictions of life. Their questions, they notice, just like the answers, can be baffling. 'In the unconscious', Freud wrote in *The Interpretation of Dreams*, 'nothing can be brought to an end, nothing is past or forgotten.' Curiosity is endless, as every parent knows, in a way that answers are not.

When Lacan asserted that the analyst was the one who was *supposed* to know, he was referring to this fact: that children take for granted, are obliged to take for granted, their parent's expertise, and that the patient, therefore, is likely to do this with the analyst. There has to be someone, somewhere, who knows and understands. That

1

is what dependence is at the beginning: entrusting oneself to the unknowable (like believing in God, or like being seduced). But the analyst, as Lacan knows, is not only the one who is supposed to know; he is the one who knows that he is supposed to know, which is to know something of extraordinary consequence – to know, as every child does somewhere, the sense in which nobody knows the answers. Childhood innocence is not naïve trust, it is incredulity (what the child has to repress is an ironic scepticism).

Adults can nurture children – there is no one else to do it – but they do not have the answers (though they are, of course, in the paradoxical position of deciding what constitutes an answer). What they can do is tell children stories about the connections between curiosity and nurture, between desire and well-being (psychoanalysis is one such story). Only the adults can provide the children with languages for their lives. Language, from the child's point of view, is always the language of experts; which is why children are prone to feeling mad when they feel themselves falling through the gaps in the language. Competence, growing up, can be about learning to keep these gaps at bay. Coherent adult practitioners must appear to know what they are saying – as though they can know something that the language they speak doesn't. Analysts can only do their work, like and unlike parents, because they know – can tell compelling stories about – what a person is, what it is to live a life, and what a life is supposed to look like. (One of their stories may be: no one is in a position to tell you that.) To walk into a psychoanalyst's consulting room, like being born into a family, is to walk into a very elaborate family of stories about who one is supposed to be. But if analysts can help patients discern the family stories they have inherited, who can help the patients, and the analysts, with the analysts' stories?

It is integral to the practice of psychoanalysis that the analyst has to fall into the trap of being treated like a parent – an authority of sorts – and then refuse to be one. Through the transference – the unwitting recreation and repetition of earlier family relationships – the analyst and the patient can reconstruct both the patient's sense of an expert, his personal picture of someone who knows best; and, perhaps more importantly, the questions, the requests, the surmises that the patient was left with as a child – the personal pantheon of demand referred to by the idea of the unconscious. By not answering the patient's questions, the analyst allows the patient both to repeat the answers of the past, and to recover the answering voices in himself. When refusing to answer questions is not traumatic for the patient – at its worst, and it is often at its worst in analysis, it merely repeats the childhood trauma of the inaccessible parent – it can reveal how someone uses other people, or what they use them for (to pre-empt the elaboration of their own thoughts, say). In other words psychoanalysis can show us how we use answers – what we are prepared to settle for – and what we use them to do. And so, by implication, it can show us what is not subject to what we call an answer, or what *may* not be – like the question, Which sex am I? In psychoanalysis, at least, answers are not a cure for questions.

The useful paradox underlying the so-called technique (and the theory) is that, in a sense, only the patient has the answers; and that the answers, in a sense, are all questions, are all requests. Knowledge is of desire – of what we want, of what we think of as missing – and desire is always in the form of a demand. To be a person is to be asking for something. Once there is dependence – once there is acknowledgement of another person as a source of satisfaction – demands are always questions: 'I want' becomes 'Can I have?' 'The subject', Lacan writes, 'has never done anything other than demand, he could not have survived otherwise; and we just follow on from there.' We are riddled by wishes and we can only survive by wanting. In the process of growing up, though, our wishes can go astray.

So how do we know – and from the child's point of view that means who can tell us – what we want? How do we know if someone is in a position to say? To tell us, for example, whether wants, supposedly like words, can be more or less true, can point us in the direction of real things?

Children's wants, at the beginning, are constituted – responded to and articulated by – the adults who look after them. They put the words to things like gestures and squeaks. The child's parents, or adult caretakers, are the arbiters of his intent, his first brush with the authorities. A baby's cries have to be interpreted, and can misfire. He may, for example, sometimes be fed when he is not hungry (and if he is always fed when he is not hungry but simply troubled, he may evolve a sense – a virtual self who believes – that what he always really wants is food). Ideally, of course, childhood is a series of reciprocal accommodations (or 'attunements' as they are now often referred to in an uneasy mixing of analogies). But however much psychoanalysts go on producing (or promoting) coercively normative accounts of good parenting – child development is the new Utopianism in psychoanalysis; it used to be normality – they cannot avoid the fact that the acquisition of language is both an innate gift and an imposition on the child. It impinges ineluctably on the child's development, making all the difference. The child may be inventive within it, but it is not the child's invention. It is, as it were, something the child has to catch; from the young child's point of view, language is what other people do; it is other people. And the learning of it will always be a paradoxical kind of trauma for the child (if not *the* paradigm of trauma itself), because the trauma can only be processed – the child will only be able to make sense of it retrospectively – in the currency of the trauma itself: in words. As though what is always part of the problem is the only solution. Language, despite its falling short, is the child's best way of wanting. But language makes desire feel like a form of compliance. To know what one wants one has to play the game.

A neurosis, in Freud's language, is a way of not knowing what one wants; as though one has learnt a language and then forgotten how to speak it. This implies, of course, that wants are knowable, that in psychoanalysis, at least, wants can be *the* objects of knowledge. We may be unacceptable to ourselves, Freud the confident Enlightenment scientist suggests, but we are not unintelligible to ourselves. After all, if we were – if our own obscurity was ineluctable – what would the analyst be doing? Pain, the psychoanalyst must believe, can be translated, like a language. The analyst can help the patient find the words. It is as though what is missing – as in infancy, or trauma – is the language, the vocabulary (though we don't tend to

4

think, in other situations, what has been added here is the language). Psychoanalysis recuperates what has been lost – not, by definition, something that never existed, something beyond words.

'From what I have so far said', Freud writes in his *Introductory Lectures*,

a neurosis would seem to be the result of a kind of ignorance – a not knowing about mental events that one ought to know of. This would be a close approximation to some well-known Socratic doctrines according to which even vices are based on ignorance.

Analogies always make a difference. Psychoanalysis is unlike Socratic dialogue in the sense that health is not necessarily akin to virtue. In psychoanalysis the opposite of ignorance is not so much knowledge (and therefore virtue) but desire (and therefore something unpredictable and morally equivocal). Freud is mapping incommensurate forms of life and language on to each other to make the kind of point that gives psychoanalysis a culturally prestigious, and therefore reassuring, affinity with classical Athens. In Vienna in the early twentieth century, knowledge was not necessarily knowledge of the good. In fact, for Freud it was the opposite. Goodness was likely to be a form of deliberate ignorance. (Parodies are always close approximations.)

But Freud's neurotic, like Socrates' bad, ignorant man, is deemed to be suffering from a refusal of knowledge. There is, it is assumed, something he is capable of knowing; he is not suffering from something that, in any absolute sense, eludes knowing. He has a capacity which, for good reasons of his own, he can't let himself use. But the patient has it in him. He is his own messenger. The analyst, like Socrates (though there must be some unconscious irony in Freud's notion of psychoanalysis as a profession of Socrateses) has to enable the patient to know what he already knows – to refind a talent, as it were. After all, the patient has only forgotten himself. And the analyst is an expert in the forms of ignorance – in the forms ignorance can take in the service of self-protection.

Or is he, rather, an expert on the inevitability of ignorance, of how we can't escape it? A want, for example, may not be something we can know, but only something we can try out – an experiment and not a fact. Psychoanalysis cannot enable the patient to know what he wants, but only to risk finding out. (In this sense perversions – states of mind in which people supposedly know exactly what they want – give knowing a bad name.) The Enlightenment Freud, like Socrates, can help us remind ourselves of who we are, of what we once and always knew (and wanted). But the post-Freudian Freud – the man who was always ahead of himself, and who we are beginning to catch up with – was the ironist of exactly this Enlightenment project.* He was an expert on the impossibility of self-knowledge, on the limits of expertise; and particularly on that version of self-knowledge that plays into the hands of instrumental reason and social control. Knowing who you are means telling people what to do.

The Enlightenment psychoanalyst knows what people need; the post-Freudian analyst knows that needs are made with words. The Enlightenment Freud ascribes needs – which he calls instincts – to people and then shows us how and why we try to disown them. The post-Freudian Freud shows us the sense in which knowing who we are – imagining ourselves, say, as made up of the relationship between two instincts, Eros and Thanatos – is only a tautology, and always an old description, because to be an expert on the unconscious is a contradiction in terms. In the mirror one always sees oneself looking.

With the Freudian version of the unconscious around, the antique injunction, know thyself, begins to beg all the questions. For how can we believe in the part of ourselves that is doing the knowing? What do we imagine the self is like – a horizon, a field, a triangle – if we can know it? And who decides what constitutes real knowledge? After the post-Freudian Freud the issue becomes not only how can we bear our (forbidden) knowledge, but how can we bear our inevitable ignorance?

The post-Freudian Freud, that is to say, was not promoting the

*I'm using these terms here as emblematic of a difference. The Enlightenment has a multiplicity of often contradictory referents now; and there is a sense in which what I am calling post-Freudian Freud is itself something made possible by so-called Enlightenment thinking.

necessity or the (traditional) value of self-doubt; he was questioning the very idea of the self as an object of knowledge (or a commodity). If a person is not a potentially knowable set of constituents – humours, faculties, predispositions, instincts – then how can we know what's missing? The inevitability of infancy, the unruliness of instinctual life, the puzzling acquisition of language and its link with sexuality, the unconscious dream-work; all of these suggested to Freud a radical and formative insufficiency, something that cannot be solved by knowledge. With the post-Freudian description of the unconscious, the idea of human completeness disappears. We are not in search of wholeness – the satisfaction, amelioration, progress, or self-knowledge of the Enlightenment Freud; we are in search of good ways of bearing our incompleteness (tragedy is when we are ruined by our insufficiency, comedy is when we can relish it). There may, sometimes, be a cure for symptoms, but there is no cure for the unconscious, no solution for unconscious desire. Knowledge can't put a stop to that, only death can.

If the Enlightenment Freud instructs us in a new science of self-knowing – of familiarizing ourselves – the post-Freudian Freud suggests that the project of self-knowledge is itself the problem, the symptom masquerading as the cure; as though we have turned the self into an object (the project of the Englightenment Freud), even an idol, and psychoanalysis can now help us to unlearn this modern religion of selfhood. The unconscious – whatever is strange, or seems foreign about ourselves – is exactly what makes our old habits of self, like knowing and understanding, sound irrelevant, off-key. An inner revisionist, it disarms our competence, like someone suddenly pointing out to us that we have been playing chess with the rules of draughts. The unconscious, in other words, is what stops self-knowledge turning, as it always does, into self-caricature (self-definition is always complicit with self-mockery). When we make a slip of the tongue, something in us speaks out of turn. It does not speak more truthfully, but it speaks as well. And at that moment we don't know where it came from. It gives us pause. In psycho-analysis, as the critic Mark Edmundson says of poetry, 'one must affirm invention at the expense of argument'.

The contemporary psychoanalyst – who must straddle both projects, contain within herself the Enlightenment Freud and the post-Freudian Freud, the knowing and the problem of knowing – becomes a new kind of expert: an expert on the truths of uncertainty. She has to recognize the sense in which each person revises – is inevitably a threat to – the available descriptions of what a person is. And psychoanalysis becomes an ironic critique, a virtual burlesque of the ethos of technology, seeing efficiency as a form of bad faith. From a psychoanalytic point of view our mistakes, our aberrations, our moments of distraction define us (inspiration is interruption): our incoherence is vital. The risk is that the contemporary psychoanalyst becomes merely a curator of paradoxes, a master of the absurdities of mastery, with all the glib Socratic trappings; wisdom as the tyranny of disingenuousness.

'The concept of the "unconscious" ', Ernest Gellner writes, 'devalues both the individual's autonomy and all inner rational compulsion, *and* the authority of evidence.' Once we have language, desire, dream-work in the picture – rather than, say, insight, mastery and empiricism – psychoanalysis becomes a primer of necessary ignorance, a reminder of the ironies of knowledge. And, therefore, the enemy of spurious alternatives. Like learning to talk for the first time, again and again.

II

Human beings have greater capacities for rote learning than horses do, a feature of the situation that, coupled with the generosity of horses, makes a lot of inadequate riding possible.
Vicki Hearne, *Tracking dogs, Sensitive Horses, and the Traces of Speech*

Psychoanalysis can never say more than language does; and no language can be the key to any other language. Just as we may take flight into inner superiority in moments of fear, we are, by the same token, prone to using authoritative, often technical languages – like psychoanalysis – in moments of awkwardness. Nothing (other than sexuality) makes people more nervous than their claims to knowledge. Special languages, like sexual techniques, are cover-ups.

For the Enlightenment Freud psychoanalysis, with its quasi-scientific terminology, was essentially about knowing. Indeed Melanie Klein believed that there was an epistemophilic *instinct* (an instinct to know), without believing that this was a contradiction in terms (or a form of terminal piety). The patient, just like the analyst, is assumed to be a proto-scientist rather than, as other parts of the theory might lead one to believe, a lover, a comedian or a mystic. He is described as being obsessed by knowing and not knowing, by thinking or refusing to think, by remembering and forgetting. In order to protect himself – to sustain a certain version of himself – he works at his ignorance.

Oedipus is so important in psychoanalysis because he does something that can be found out, something he can know about. The Oedipus plays would be a very different theatrical experience if everybody was walking round the stage completely baffled all the time (how would it end?). The fictional Oedipus becomes the paradigmatic seeker and avoider of truth, and therefore the sustainer of the idea that there are truths. He is a man lucky or unlucky enough to have a truth to discover, the man who fails at repression. (We know nothing, of course, about the successfully repressed; what would psychoanalysis be if Oedipus had got away with it?) If knowledge means evidence of a crime committed, and the self is essentially a criminal, then both are intelligible. Once a crime has been committed, the question 'Why is it better to know the truth?' and the answer 'It's impossible to know whether it will be better or not' seem merely evasive, or churlish. The value of knowing, and the moral disgrace of concealment, at least in the context of the plays and the law-court, seem self-evident (though comedy can celebrate where tragedy can only punish). After all, what else can we do with crimes – and with people – but find them out? The idea of truth makes us virtuous, shows us which side to be on; it makes it possible for us to blame, to forgive and to punish.

But one of the consequences of privileging Oedipus, as Freud did, is that the psychoanalyst then assumes that the patient's real genre is tragedy, and that his real project is knowledge or understanding. It is, though, part of the patient's predicament that he is trapped in a specific genre, that he is unable to move freely among the genres available; his farces, say, are all experienced as tragedies. And, of course, every child notices that there is a hunger for more than knowledge; and hopefully every adult patient notices that the sexual pleasures of insight are rather different from the sexual pleasures of sex. If Oedipus is a tragedy, the analyst can help the patient to know; if Oedipus is a black comedy – and the naïvety of the main protagonists *is* truly staggering – the analyst may be less sure of his role. Knowing is not quite the same as getting the joke. And a comic, of course, is not an expert on jokes, only at telling them. After all, what would we need an expert on jokes for? What can we add to a joke that will make it better? The risk is that the Enlightenment Freud ruins the joke by explaining it. Nobody reads 'Jokes and Their Relation to the Unconscious' for the jokes.

Once Freud had made Oedipus the tragic hero of psychoanalysis – not a screen-memory, not a dream still to be interpreted, not the failed initiate of Jean-Joseph Goux's account, but a kind of absolute referent – there was a sense in which he could know what he was doing. He could be a detective and a doctor, the benign unraveller of plots; a protector of the well-being of the state. Indeed, without the Oedipus complex, without incestuous desire, the Freudian unconscious doesn't make sense; the unacceptable has to start somewhere, and it is incest that sets it off.

And yet, of course, that is the point about the unconscious: it doesn't make sense. With the unconscious you never know where you are. For the Enlightenment Freud, paradoxically, the Oedipus complex makes the unconscious intelligible; it gives it a discernible function, and a master-plot to keep the story going, the story of our forbidden life. Incestuous desire gives an origin, a source, for the idea of forbidden knowledge (and Oedipus becomes our pioneer in this dangerous territory). With the Oedipus story as a foundation – Oedipus as a kind of early scientific hero – psychoanalysis could be the science of the forbidden, of the unacceptable; and the neurotic could be a failed scientist. With Freud's rediscovery of Oedipus, in fact, a new version of the good life was being described. In Freud's view – and this is one of his fundamental models for a life – the criminal must become a scientist. Crime doesn't pay, but knowledge does. In so far as the Oedipus complex is the truth of our being – and it is surely impossible to imagine that it is not at least one constitutive story for imagining ourselves – the psychoanalyst becomes a kind of expert witness.

From criminality to science, with the artist as a go-between: this was the drama that the psychoanalyst – not only a new professional, but a new kind of person invented by Freud – was to contain. In so far as he believed in development, in a myth of progress, he was to be a scientist. And yet, as psychoanalysis itself reminds us, now more than ever before, people were babies before they became addicted to knowing – and before they became those hardened (Oedipal) criminals, always guilty until proved guilty. The patient who comes into the analyst's consulting room, always comes because he cannot speak; he began his life without words, surrounded by them. He comes not only as someone refusing knowledge, but as someone for whom, once, there was no such thing. It is not common enough knowledge that everyone was originally a baby.

So any form of expertise – and especially psychoanalysis, with its constitutive wish to link bodies to their words – is going to recreate that crisis of authority and knowledge that is at the heart of both infancy and the acquisition of language (and later, of the Oedipus complex). The act of knowing – as opposed, say, to the capacity to be absorbed in someone or something – is itself more of a problem than what there is to know. (Or rather, the problem of knowing is hidden by the vividness of its objects.) There is life before knowledge, and somebody before words. And every life is constituted through the generations that precede it, like an obscured inheritance ('Our simple childhood', Wordworth writes in Book V of *The Prelude*, 'sits upon a throne/That hath more power than all the elements'). The crucial things happened to Oedipus – instigated his plot, as it were – before his birth and when he was a baby (his parents' own history, the oracle, his abandonment, etc.). Like everybody else, Oedipus, even at the end of his ordeal, could not be an expert on, or the originator of, his own life; he could only live it, only see it proliferating (choice is also the retrospective word for chance). Describing people as the (sole) authors of their own lives is another way of punishing them.

It is, of course, part of the legacy of psychoanalysis to make Oedipus seem intelligible (a psychoanalyst might say to Oedipus: live as you would be lived by). But what can psychoanalysis bring to the story now that would make Oedipus unfathomable, as he was to himself? How could psychoanalysis add to his passion? At its worst psychoanalysis seems to make the play redundant, superseded by its interpretation (there could be as many readings of the play as there are people). But it is the Enlightenment Freud that always pushes for consensus, that is willing a community of more or less shared knowledge (which might now be called a psychoanalytic training institute, or a group of apparently like-minded people). At the end of the Oedipus plays the audience and the protagonists come to some shared understanding of what has happened (meaning requires accomplices). By the end we are all experts, though, in a sense, nothing has been explained. Why would someone want to have sex with their mother? What is curiosity? Where do the important questions come from?

The psychoanalyst is an expert on the ways in which the patient pretends to be an expert on himself; the ways, that is, in which he gravitates towards consensus, to fitting in. The Enlightenment Freud wants to tell us what we have in common; the post-Freudian Freud, his collaborative antagonist, is the connoisseur of anomalies. He shows us the whys and wherefores of denying difference, and particularly one's difference from oneself. Dreams are his exemplary objects – not theories or facts – because they are at once partially intelligible and unsharable in their original form (other people only know the story of our dream). And dreams cannot be measured.

III

God made everything out of nothing. But the nothing shows through.

Paul Valéry, *Oeuvres II*

The Enlightenment Freudian has two obvious areas of expertise. He knows the range of possible blind spots, the cultural repertoire of unacceptable and forbidden things, like incestuous desire and violence. And he knows how and why people create and sustain their blind spots, how they guarantee their ignorance. All the defences that Freud and others have described – denial, repression, splitting, projection, turning a blind eye, and so on – are made, of course, out of prior acknowledgements – of dangers, or muddles registered as threats. The question for the Enlightenment psychoanalyst – the Socratic analyst – is, How does the patient's ignorance work, and how come it is felt to be necessary? What is it deemed better not to know, and who has decided that (someone may have put the patient up to it)?

One problem for the patient is that the Enlightenment psychoanalyst has already decided, broadly speaking, what the patient thinks it is better not to know. Indeed, each psychoanalytic theorist, starting with Freud, describes a set of essential terrors; that which, it is assumed, people cannot bear to remember, experience, or know. These essential terrors define what it is to be human; or what, in order to be human, one feels obliged to exclude. Psychoanalytic theory is a theory of the unbearable, of what one prefers not to know. For Freud the unbearable is the castration born of incestuous desire; for Jones it is Aphinisis, the death of desire; for Klein, the tyranny of the death instinct; for Winnicott impingement and being dropped; for Bion the impossibility of making links; for Lacan, semiotic collapse, and so on. Either we are suffering from something supposedly intrinsic to being human – incestuous desire, a death instinct, dependence – or our earliest environment, our formative relationships, have made our putative nature problematic for us. Usually, nowadays, it is construed as a mêlée of both: nature and nurture as mutually disfiguring, with ambivalence as Freud's cure for the tyrannies of perfection.

But as each theorist offers us a new redescription of the unacceptable – of what we are suffering from, of what we have to fear – they become, by the same token, the masters of our suffering. By punctuating our unhappiness, they make it legible. Like religious or political leaders, they tell us persuasive stories about where the misery comes from, and hence, by implication, what we might do about it. They want to change our (and their) relationship to the fear they have formulated for us. The expert constructs the terror, and then the terror makes the expert. If you are part of the solution, you are part of the problem. Experts, in other words, can give us descriptions that allow us to be unhappy in new ways.

In so far as there is a complicity between terrors and experts – and how could there not be? – then the Enlightenment Freud is part of the problem. ('The famine's everywhere there's UNICEF', as Frederick Seidel writes in his poem 'Recessional'.) But the Freud that has given us the conceptual tools to dismantle the Enlightenment project of efficient knowledge – the unconscious, the dream-work, the transference – has also given us, those of us who are impressed by his words, a double message: he tells us the truth about ourselves, and then asks us why we believe him. He tells us a story about ourselves and then he tells us a story about how come we are such avid listeners to stories. By showing us the childhood origins of belief – the terrors that prompt our need, as children, for experts – he makes us wonder about the provenance of belief itself. As though to be human is to be addicted not to beliefs but to believing. The post-Freudian psychoanalyst analyses the patient's will to believe.

The infant, of course, does not believe, or believe in, his parents; he takes their authority, their nurture, for granted. ('Belief', Freud wrote to Fleiss in 1897, '. . . has no counterpart in the unconscious.') The Oedipal child, who needs his parents' love and protection, cannot have a sexual relationship with his parents, but he can do the next best thing – he can believe them. As every fan knows, credulity is a sexual act; faith is a form of longing. From a psychoanalytic point of view the question is not only, What is the expert – the parent, the psychoanalyst, the star – saying? but, Why do we believe him, what makes us?

Belief, as Freud shows, domesticates desire. Experts keep us on their best behaviour.

IV

The madman is not the man who has lost his reason. The
madman is the man who has lost everything except his reason.
G. K. Chesterton, *Orthodoxy*

Freud's description of the unconscious suggests that we are lost in thought, and yet people come for psychoanalysis to find out where, or who, they are. The Enlightenment Freudian can help them with their orienteering, but with the post-Freudian Freud they are likely to be at cross purposes. Adults, after all, don't tend to go out with the intention of getting lost (though it's not obvious why they don't). Nor do people want to pay good money to realize how clueless they are. Being all over the place, or being seen to be, is traditionally considered to be something of a drawback. Symptoms, like insights – pieces of self-knowledge – at least allow one to identify oneself, to make 'I am the kind of person who . . .' statements. But if, as Freud suggests, to 'have' an unconscious is to be, or to make oneself radically odd to oneself – to be always in and out of character – what is the analyst supposed to be doing to (or for) his patients? To make them more knowing, or enable them to tolerate, or take pleasure from, their clouds of unknowing? Show them that they are afloat on their ignorance, buoyant sometimes, or help them swim for shore? 'To improve society spend/more time with people you haven't/met', John Cage advises. You can't help but do this, Freud says, because the person one hasn't met is also always oneself.

For Freud, to be a person is to be a stranger to oneself – quite literally, to be continually meeting oneself as though one was somebody else ('The foreigner', Edmond Jabès writes, 'allows you to be yourself by making a foreigner of you'). What is surprising is how unsurprised we are by ourselves (we comfort ourselves by simulating repetitions). 'All the acts and manifestations which I notice in myself', Freud writes in *The Unconscious*, 'and do not know how to link up with the rest of my mental life must be judged as if they belonged to someone else.' 'As if' because, of course, they don't belong to someone else; one has had to turn oneself into a stranger, into another apparently unrecognizable person, to make one's life psychically viable. Self-estrangement, Freud shows, protects us from a threatening affinity with all we have tried to disown. Everything that seems remote or bizarre is too close for comfort. ('What is experienced as uncanny', Freud writes in his paper on the subject, 'can be traced back without exception to something familiar that has been repressed.') Nothing that is human is alien, but nothing that is human can do without the idea of the alien, to protect itself.

For the Enlightenment Freud the project is one of retranslation; of re-acquainting patients with themselves, of humanizing their gods. The analyst is a reminder. The repressed unconscious may be an uninvited guest, but the patient can learn inner hospitality. The psychoanalyst is not, then, an expert on strangers – after all, what would it be to be an expert on strangers? – but an expert on how and why people turn themselves into strangers (metamorphosis is another word for being on the run). Patients, in fact, could not be more familiar with themselves. The analyst, like a good host, just goes on making the introductions. This is not always a pleasant task but it is not, necessarily, an impossible one. The repressed unconscious is at least potentially knowable, along the lines of the Englightenment principle that what we have made – laws, constitutions, the repressed – we must know and can remake. Nothing a person makes, including his character, is fixed. It is here that psychoanalysis joins with its precursor, the nineteenth-century European novel (Freud's ego being a fictional character like, say, Stendhal's Julien Sorel).

But if one source of strangeness, in Freud's view, is the unacceptable – made strange, defamiliarized, as a defensive measure – the other source, less amenable to psychoanalytic (or any other) description, is what might be called the unintelligible: whatever in our experience does not seem subject to our sense-making; whatever baffles, or inspires *because* it baffles, our powers of representation. This other unconscious – that which is out of bounds, but not by law (repression), like the fact of one's infancy, or the fact of one's forthcoming death, or the future itself – is a way of describing both the limits of what we can know and the areas of our lives in which knowing, and the idea of expertise, may be inappropriate. The unacceptable, to some extent, can be known; the unintelligible can only be acknowledged. By transgressing, we find the forbidden; there is no equivalent way of finding the other privacies. Another way of saying this is that the art of psychoanalysis is knowing what not to interpret. The risk is that the psychoanalyst won't know when to leave the patient alone.

The psychoanalyst aims for the spoken, aims, as R. P. Blackmur said of poetry, 'to add to the stock of available reality'. The Enlightenment Freud and his patient are accumulating cultural capital, insuring themselves against the future with insight. The post-Freudian Freud and his patient are making a provisional investment, gambling on uncertainty. Heir to both projects, the contemporary analyst, like her patient, can never know what it is possible to say, nor the consequences of that saying. What we are asking for can be a surprise.

1

Authorities

I

Remaining serious is successful repression.

Sándor Ferenczi, *Laughter*

There has always been a resistance, at least among psychoanalysts themselves, to thinking of their work as mind-reading or fortune-telling. Despite the fact that most ordinary conversation is exactly this, or perhaps because it is, psychoanalysts have wanted to describe what they do as different, as rational, even – dealing with the irrational but not dealing in it. ('On waking', Ferenczi writes mockingly to Freud, 'one wants on no account to have thought something quite nonsensical or illogical.') It was important to Freud that psychoanalysis should not become a cult of the irrational. The unconscious may be disreputable, but the psychoanalyst must not be. And yet Freud's description of the unconscious was a threat to, and a parody of, the more respectable versions of professional competence. If a psychoanalyst knows what's in the unconscious, or knows how it works, she has a specific expertise. But if the unconscious is what cannot be anticipated, how can there be experts of the unknown? 'The weather', as Freud puts it in an early letter to Ferenczi, his Hungarian disciple, 'of course never comes from the quarter one has been carefully observing.'

Located somewhere between literature and science, psychoanalysis can begin to look like a legitimate and intelligible social practice – not so much a mystery for initiates but a skill that can be learned, with real rules and a body of knowledge. Like the so-called neurotic, whose project is to be extremely normal, psychoanalysis has always struggled to distance itself from supposedly discredited things like religion, glamour, mysticism, radical politics, the paranormal, and all the scapegoated 'alternative' therapies. Psychoanalysis, that is to say, has used its discovery of the unconscious to legitimate itself. This would once have been called an irony. Psychoanalysis as a treatment may be about reclaiming the marginalized parts of oneself, but psychoanalysis as a profession has always been resolutely committed to the mainstream, which at the moment happens to be science and various literary theories of narrative. So it is perhaps not entirely surprising that psychoanalysis has been especially dissmissive of – has, indeed, pathologized – what was once referred to as the supernatural. From the extraordinary correspondence between Freud and Ferenczi, which radically changes the way we read psychoanalysis – letters give us the unofficial history of psychoanalysis – it is clear that sexuality and the unconscious were the new, scientifically prestigious words for the occult, for that which is beyond our capacity for knowledge, for the weird, unaccountable effects people have on each other. In psychoanalysis the supernatural returns as the erotic. It was Ferenczi, and Jung in a different way, who had to keep reminding Freud of the limits of scientific enquiry; that to rationalize the unconscious was an aim, but also a betrayal, of psychoanalysis. When Ferenczi wrote to Freud in 1911 that he 'considered the fight against occultism to be premature', he was trying to keep alive something he saw as integral to the psychoanalytic project – something that might be called inexplicable human powers – and which Freud, in Ferenczi's view, was too keen to disavow.

If the aim of a system is to create an outside where you can put the things you don't want, then we have to look at what that system disposes of – its rubbish – to understand it, to get a picture of how it sees itself and wants to be seen. The proscribed vocabulary in anybody's theory is as telling as the recommended vocabulary (insouciance and recklessness, for example, are not psychoanalytic terms in the way that trust and integration are). Freud had apparently included sex and violence in the science of psychoanalysis, but he balked at the investigation of occult phenomena. If sexuality was the unacceptable in psychoanalysis, then what kind of sexuality was the occult, proscribed by the master of the forbidden himself? (One answer, as we shall see, is homosexuality.) Ferenczi, as Freud wrote in a foreword to a collection of his papers, was 'familiar to an extent that few others are with all the difficulties of psychoanalytic problems'. In the letters, unlike the theoretical papers, it is as though Ferenczi is Freud's repressed unconscious – the prodigal son who keeps coming back for more – wittingly and unwittingly drawing Freud's attention to the implications of psychoanalytic theory that Freud preferred to forget, partly because they were, inevitably, connected to all the difficulties of his own problems. Intimacy between people, like occult phenomena, is fundamentally bewildering. Freud, as Ferenczi knew, was cautious about passion in his personal life and about mysticism in his professional life. (Mysticism, after all, is knowledge that by definition exempts itself from legitimation.) If psychoanalysis, for Ferenczi, was a way of dispelling the secrecy between people, it was also a way of having an intimate relationship with Freud (Ferenczi did, of course, have two brief analyses with Freud). But Freud, unlike Ferenczi, was a lover of secrets, and believed that they should not be squandered, or allowed to become some spurious currency of intimacy. For Freud, that is to say, psychoanalysis was also a tribute to the unspoken. 'Don't sacrifice too many of your secrets', he warns Ferenczi, 'out of an excess of kindness.' The sacrificing of secrets was a virtual definition of psychoanalysis, though it was not always clear which gods were being propitiated.

II

Is it possible (?) to make friends with the unconscious?
Sándor Ferenczi, *Notes and Fragments*

Freud, Ferenczi had written in one of his early papers, 'had succeeded in surprising a process . . . in taking it in the midst of its work, in flagrante, so to speak'. Dreaming was the process in question; Ferenczi clearly liked the idea of Freud as the man who found things out, the transgressor of privacy. But from a psychoanalytic point of view that Ferenczi would never quite accept, human beings were the animals that kept secrets (this was one of the things Freud meant by the idea of the unconscious). Ferenczi always wanted to get to the bottom of such things, so to speak. And the secrets of sexuality that Freud had discovered were inextricably linked, for him, with the mysteries of more traditional, folkloric forms of magic. Of course a lot of 'artists and intellectuals', not to mention ordinary people, at the turn of the century were interested in what was then called, to give it scientific credibility, psychical research. Freud himself had been made an honorary member of the Society for Psychical Research in 1911, but he was wary, as his correspondence with Ferenczi makes clear, of psychoanalysis being associated with the fringes of science. He preferred to think of psychoanalysis as a medical treatment rather than a seance. But despite Freud's misgivings, Ferenczi went to visit a medium, Frau Seidler, after their trip to America in 1909, with Freud's full endorsement. He went 'with the intention', the editors of their correspondence write calmly, 'of investigating parapsychological phenomena', as if we might be suspicious of his real motives (as in, Ferenczi bought pornography 'with the intention of investigating erotic phenomena'). Immediately reporting the outcome enthusiastically to Freud, the intrepid conquistador of the other mysteries is 'shocked'. 'Keep quiet about it for the time being', Freud counsels Ferenczi. In his next letter, written five days later, Freud has, as it were, changed his mind: 'let us keep absolute silence about it . . . should one now, as a result of this experience, commit oneself to occultism? Certainly not; it is only a matter of thought transference.' But what, then, is thought transference, and how does it work? The vocabulary for one mysterious form of exchange merely replaces another. And what has happened to the honesty (a key word in this correspondence), the spirit of open scientific enquiry that Freud and psychoanalysis had prided itself on? The psychoanalyst could protect himself from sexuality, but he might not be able to resist the contamination of the paranormal.

But Ferenczi, who planned a book on thought transference which he never wrote, was beginning to discover something in his clinical work that the peculiar practices of psychics helped him to think about – something that it has taken psychoanalysts virtually until now to fully appreciate (or rather, to face). Ferenczi was finding that sometimes his own free-associations to the patient's material seemed to be of a piece with what the patient was saying to him, as though the analyst might be having some of the patient's (repressed) thoughts for him – continuing them, as it were. The analyst therefore became a medium, in a slightly different sense of the word, for the thoughts and feelings the patient could not bear. The patient could evoke in the analyst, as though by thought transference, the disowned parts of himself. (It is, in fact, a common experience in ordinary conversation: people speak each other's disowned voices.) Parapsychological phenomena made crudely vivid, the fact that there was a kind of hidden exchange of psychic states going on between people, a black market of feelings that was not subject to conscious control. And it was obvious to Ferenczi that if this was true, then it was going to be a two-way traffic: it couldn't only be the patient doing this to the analyst; it must also be the analyst doing it to the patient. This made psychoanalysis a rather more reciprocal venture than Freud's resolutely scientific, quasi-medical model could allow. When two people speak to each other, they soon become inextricable: words are contagious. As Freud and Ferenczi went on speaking to each other, they needed to find theories about what happens when people speak (and listen) to each other to manage the intensity of the experience. It was as though Freud had invented the psychoanalytic relationship as a refuge from intimacy – a place it could be studied, a relationship about intimacy but not 'really' intimate itself – and Ferenczi was determinedly showing him that there was no talk without intimacy or its refusal.

It is no accident that, as their relationship evolves in the years covered by this correspondence, Freud and Ferenczi begin to write about the connections between homosexuality and paranoia, (between sameness and difference). In 1911 Freud published his Schreber case ('I am Schreber, nothing but Schreber,' Freud writes to Ferenczi); and Ferenczi published *On the Part Played by Homosexuality in the Pathogenesis of Paranoia* (1912) and his remarkable paper, *The Nosology of Male Homosexuality* (1914). Towards the end of the correspondence Freud published a provisional summation of all this in *Totem and Taboo*, in which Ferenczi praises ingenuously Freud's 'new and outstanding idea of transmission by means of unconscious understanding', an idea that Ferenczi had been 'carrying' for Freud for several years, an idea derived from parapsychology. As the editors of their correspondence for these years put it, hopefully with unconscious irony, 'Freud and Ferenczi did more work together than has sometimes been acknowledged.' Theory, as psychoanalysis shows, is always first and foremost local emotional politics. 'If psychoanalysis is a paranoia', Ferenczi writes jokingly to Freud, 'then I have already been successful in overcoming the stage of persecution mania and replacing it with megalomania.'

If psychoanalysis is a paranoia, then it is, in the terms of its own theory, a love between men. 'Paranoia', as Ferenczi wrote, more or less echoing Freud, 'is perhaps nothing else at all but disguised homosexuality.' There is something so unbearable about love for one's own sex that it is turned into hatred, and the hatred is then projected into other people and comes back from outside as persecution. In fact Ferenczi believed that men adored women to protect themselves from their love for men; so the men then hated the women because they weren't men and the women felt inadequate, unable to satisfy their men or themselves. 'I quite seriously believe', Ferenczi wrote in *The Nosology of Male Homosexuality*, 'that the men of today are obsessively heterosexual as the result of this affective displacement; in order to free themselves from men, they become the slaves of women.' But what is it in men that men are so much on the run from? This was the question that Ferenczi implicitly addressed to Freud, sometimes as theory, and sometimes as a direct appeal to Freud for a different, less careful intimacy.

Despite Freud's commitment, in theory, to bisexuality – love, hate and rivalry with *both* parents – it was more or less assumed in psychoanalysis (and still is in some quarters) that if all goes well, heterosexuality wins the day. For example, in psychoanalytic theory love for the parent of the opposite sex is referred to as the positive Oedipus complex and love for the parent of the same sex is called the negative Oedipus complex. It is, in other words, quite clear what we are supposed to be doing. But as Ferenczi intimates in his letters and his 'scientific' papers, heterosexuality is, among other things, a form of self-hatred – what is so distasteful about one's own sex that one has, so exclusively, to desire the opposite one? The interesting link that psychoanalysis had constructed between paranoia and homosexuality revealed something even more disquieting which Freud and Ferenczi could never quite formulate: that in psychoanalysis, at least, heterosexuality was a form of redemption from a profound, perhaps constitutive self-fear. In theory psychoanalysis promoted the value, indeed the necessity, of love for both sexes. Unlike Freud, Ferenczi wanted to try to live out – or act out, as psychoanalysts would say disparagingly – the consequences of psychoanalytic theory, and in part with Freud himself. Or, as the editor says in his sensible Introduction to the first volume of their correspondence, Ferenczi 'made little clear or defensive distinction between his professional life and his private life'. The unconscious does not have a professional life. Except, that is, in psychoanalysis.

Ferenczi proposed the new term 'ambisexuality' instead of the term 'bisexuality' to stress the novelty of the psychoanalytic version of this ancient idea. In his view it better described the child's actual predicament: 'the child's psychical capacity for bestowing his erotism, originally objectless, on either the male or the female sex, or on both'. The translator's word 'bestow' sounds quaint now, but it accurately captures the sense of desire as something conferred. For the child, like the adult, desire is experienced as a gift: we privilege people with our desire for them, though they don't always recognize quite what an honour they are being given. As the letters show with amazing candour, Ferenczi bestowed his remarkable child-like capacity for intimacy on Freud, and Freud responded with a wariness and a generosity no less passionate, although never quite passionate or open enough for Ferenczi. 'You actually do feel best', Ferenczi writes to Freud, as compliment and reproach, 'when you can be independent of the whole world.' Inevitably both of them were confronted, as in a psychoanalysis, with the question of what they wanted from each other, which brought with it the question that was to haunt psychoanalysis: Should wants be understood or met? In Freud's view, psychoanalysis was defined as a treatment in which wants could be thought about and not pre-empted by being gratified. In Ferenczi's version of psychoanalysis, to frustrate the patient too much was to recreate in the treatment exactly the childhood trauma that necessitated the treatment in the first place. This issue of whether a want is something that can be satisfied or whether in and of itself it spells the impossibility of satisfaction – the necessary gap between desire and its object – was one of the many contentions that bound Freud and Ferenczi together, and set the terms for the future of psychoanalytic debate. Does desire, at its best, mature into thought (and theory), or is it the other way round? Their correspondence, like the theoretical work written between 1908 and 1914 (forty works by Freud and fifty-six by Ferenczi), is a record of the inspiring turbulence they evoked in each other from the beginning, in which issues of truth and honesty were bound up with the apparently theoretical question of homosexuality; a record of the feelings two men might have for each other (in the context of other significant relationships). It is rare to be able to read such theoretical love letters, a genre of course, traditionally associated with fantasies of truth-telling.

III

Do not force feelings of any kind, least of all the feeling of conviction.

Sándor Ferenczi, *Notes and Fragments*

For Ferenczi, seventeen years younger than Freud, and more emotionally extravagant than Freud, psychoanalysis was useful as a way of thinking about what he called his 'ideal of honesty'. 'Not everything that is infantile should be abhorred,' he writes to Freud in the early years of their relationship, 'for example the child's urge for truth, which is only dammed up by false educational influences . . . I still hold firmly to the conviction that it is not honesty but superfluous secrecy that is abnormal' – an intimation of the superfluous secrecy between Freud and himself. In Ferenczi's view, the child is an instinctive truth-teller potentially perverted by adult conspiracies. 'Many intelligent children', he writes in an early paper (*Transitory Symptom Constructions during the Analysis*, 1912),

at the stage of repression marked by the latency period, before they have gone through 'the great intimidation', regard adults as dangerous fools, to whom one cannot tell the truth without running the risk of being punished for it: and whose inconsistencies and follies have to be taken into consideration. In this children are not so very wrong.

From the child's point of view, parents can be occult phenomena. Children, and the adults they will become, suffer from their parents' inability, or unwillingness, to acknowledge their truth. Adults may not be able to answer the child's questions, but they can take them as warranting consideration. In Ferenczi's view, the adults cannot be trusted. But psychoanalysis itself might make us wonder, What is the picture we have of ourselves that makes the idea of trust so important? Modern stories about childhood – like psychoanalysis – are riddled with superstitions about trust: as though trust was a ground for truth, or that what we do with our words is trust them.

For Freud, of course, it wasn't that children told the truth, it was that they desired their parents. So is desiring, as Ferenczi implies, a way of telling the truth? Or is this belief in truth, at least in a psychoanalytic context, a noble and innocent – noble because innocent – cover story for the forbidden mess of desire? Freud believed that children lived the truth about sex; Ferenczi believed that children spoke the truth about truth. It was as if 'original virtue' was being smuggled back into psychoanalysis – Rousseau returning through the back door. Because if there is a Freudian unconscious, what exactly is this truth that the child has an 'urge' for? 'Super-fluous secrecy' could just be a way of describing the repressed unconscious of Freudian Man. What Ferenczi never quite spells out is what the child wants from telling the so-called truth; that would be the Freudian question. In so far as childhood, in Ferenczi's version, is a state of submission, the fault lies fairly and squarely with the parents, and children are virtually robbed of their intrinsically problematic nature.

At its best Ferenczi's work is saying something that has come to seem very important: children grow by being listened to; adults are frightened of listening to children because of what they might feel as a consequence; some secrets in the family turn children into sleepwalkers; parents are extraordinary to children. But at its worst children are burdened with a quasi-oracular status that they cannot make sense of, or bear responsibility for. Fantasies of truth, after all, are adult constructions, something children learn from the adult world. Children are not naturally anything, other than the adult's construction of their nature. But these issues, as discussed by Freud and Ferenczi, are part of the origins of the contemporary debate about child sexual abuse. Ferenczi's 'ideal of honesty', which is a recurrent theme in these letters, alerted psychoanalysts to the senses in which interpretation can be a refusal to listen, and to the fact that believing the patient, which means believing in the patient, is integral to the successful process of analysis and, more importantly, is a fundamental form of kindness. 'The admission of the analyst's error', Ferenczi noted in his essential paper of 1933, 'Confusion of Tongues', 'produced confidence in his patient'. Concealing shame sabotages intimacy.

But in what sense does believing what people say entail agreeing with them, and how do I know if I've believed what someone says to me? If I hear something they don't hear in what they say, am I then disbelieving them? Freud, in a way that Ferenczi could not always acknowledge, ineluctably complicated these notions of truth and belief. In fact one of the implications of Freudian theory was that the idea of truth, as some consensual superordinate idol – as something around which we might all agree – could be a coercive attempt to deny differences. Ferenczi, at various points in this correspondence, suggests that psychoanalysis, with its promise of free speech, might itself be a unifying force.

Freud, however, experienced his younger colleague's ideal of honesty as the more complicated appeal that it in fact was. Characteristically, Freud picked up the demand in Ferenczi's often expressed wish for openness and honesty. 'Just think what it would mean', Ferenczi wrote to Freud in 1910, 'if one could tell everyone the *truth*, one's father, teacher, neighbour, and even the king. All fabricated, imposed authority would go to the devil – what is rightful would remain natural.' Ferenczi understood like nobody else, even Freud perhaps, the revolutionary potential of psychoanalysis. He knew that people speaking differently to each other changes the world (it is noticeable, though, that the people he wants to speak the truth to, in so far as they are explicitly gendered, are men). Ferenczi doesn't tell us why or how being able to tell everyone the truth – whatever one conceives that to be – would destroy those forms of oppressive authority. But it is as if Freud, in his reply to this letter, hears this as a wish, which it must also have been, for freer talk between the two of them. Freud was certainly, as Ferenczi was quick to tell him, father, teacher, and king to him. 'I feel myself to be a match for anything', Freud replies cannily, 'and approve of the overcoming of my homosexuality, with the result being greater independence.' For Freud, freedom, at least consciously, was in overcoming, silencing his homosexual self; for Ferenczi, independence would be in its free expression. Freud sensed, I think, that Ferenczi's fantasy of honesty, of people saying anything and everything to each other, was also a fantasy of symbiosis, of there being no differences between people (if we tell each other everything, it is as though we never leave each other out). And yet, in psychoanalytic treatment, one can begin to understand how speaking freely has become a mortal danger for someone. Saying whatever comes into one's mind was something Freud believed one should do in analysis; Ferenczi wanted the psychoanalytic relationship to be the paradigm for social relations. But it would have to be a version of psychoanalysis in which the analyst could tell the patient whatever was on his mind as well. Mutual interpretation, and mutual free-association. No kings.

What was homosexuality for Freud, we are obliged to wonder now, if he needed to 'overcome' it to sustain his independence? It often seems as though Freud experiences Ferenczi, in their correspondence, at least, as both the son trying to seduce the father and the son trying to turn the father into a mother. Unsubtly, Ferenczi refers in a letter to Jung's wife talking of Freud's 'antipathy toward giving completely of yourself as a friend'. Was Freud anxious about intimacy, as Ferenczi often implies in this correspondence, or was it that Ferenczi couldn't tolerate the differences between them – differences of generation and temperament, different ways of loving? And what was the self imagined to be if it could be given completely (the self as gift is integral to modern stories about the self)? Difference or defensiveness has always been a dilemma that psychoanalysis has been unable to deal with. Is the patient different from the analyst's description of him, or merely resistant to the analyst's interpretation? And who is in a position to decide? If one way of talking about these perplexing issues, albeit guardedly, was to theorize about homosexuality, the other less contentious way was to talk about the women in their lives. Or rather, for the younger man to talk to Freud about the women in their lives. Mrs Freud was another of Freud's secrets.

As in all Freud's correspondence, the men tend to flex their psychoanalytic muscles over the women. The psychoanalytic 'movement' is always an invigoratingly fraught subject around which they can divide and bond, but it is as though they have the women in common, as a problem they can huddle over. Managing the women – Freud, for example, refers in a letter to Lou Andreas-Salome as 'a woman of dangerous intelligence' – and the so-called heretics kept Freud's psychoanalytic group together. The drama of Freud's and Ferenczi's relationship in their correspondence is fed by the well-known drama of Jung's dissension, and the less notorious drama of Ferenczi's love affair with an older woman, Gizella, his mistress and future wife, and her daughter Elma, who was Ferenczi's, and later Freud's, analysand. Ferenczi was briefly engaged to Elma, who eventually married someone else. Jung, as Freud's and Ferenczi's letters show, was clearly scapegoated as an occultist and anti-semite; which, whether he was both those things or not, says something about what the psychoanalytic group used him for. And Ferenczi's professional reputation was to be retrospectively disparaged because of his supposed emotional and erotic instability. When it came to radically dissenting views, and unusual ways of living, the psychoanalytic group – not for the last time – showed itself to be expert at character assassination. The unconscious was not allowed to be a counter-culture. It had to be assimilated.

In their early letters, we see Ferenczi trying to cure himself of Freud, but sustain his relationship with him. Jung, Ferenczi writes to Freud in 1912, 'identifies confession with psychoanalysis and evidently doesn't know that the confession of sins is the lesser task of psychoanalytic therapy: the greater one is *the demolition of the father imago*, which is completely absent in confession.' Ferenczi realized that the future of psychoanalysis depended upon analysts understanding their relationship with – their transference to – Freud himself. (People sometimes kill fathers when they can't do anything else with them.) Freud, after all, had done a very paradoxical thing: he had invented a form of authority, the science of psychoanalysis, as a treatment that depended on demolishing forms of authority. It was to be a double bind that drove people mad – either crazily conformist or crazily bizarre. 'I had to observe not without pain', Ferenczi writes to Freud after their holiday together in 1914, 'that my position with respect to you, specifically, is still not completely natural, and that your presence arouses inhibitions of various kinds in me that influence, and at times almost paralyse, my actions and even my thinking.' It takes two to create this kind of unease.

Freud treats Ferenczi, in their correspondence, as though Ferenczi was someone who was always prone to over-react. And yet Freud's *Studies in Hysteria* had shown the senses in which it was impossible for a person to over-react. This, indeed, was one of the radical things about Freud's work: it legitimated his patient's responses to their predicaments by making them intelligible. When Freud asserted, in his *New Introductory Lectures*, that the patient's symptoms *were* his sexual life, he was speaking up for the inventiveness, the resourcefulness of his patient's sexuality; that we are at our most articulate in our sexuality, because we are at our most puzzling. Ferenczi, a bit like one of the so-called hysterics that Freud treated, made the difficult demands on psychoanalysis and its discoverer that would be the source of its future vitality. (After all, what would psychoanalysis do without the symptoms it can't cure?) How could two people sit in a room together talking and go on believing that one was more authoritative than the other? Why would a person want to understand someone, or even cure them, rather than have sex with them? In what sense are psychoanalytic techniques complicit with the traumas they were invented to treat? ('A neglected motive for "identification" is imitation as a contemptuous grimace', Ferenczi notes towards the end of his life.) What happens to our aspirations to competence – our fantasies of perfection – if we begin to live as though there is an unconscious? How could one protect a person's best interests by being unfriendly to them? Psychoanalytic theory, as Ferenczi knew, made these questions unavoidable. Psychoanalytic institutions tended to rule them out of court.

As Ferenczi knew, psychoanalytic trainings are always potentially paralysed – indeed, judging by their piety, terrorized – by their excessive regard for the older generations. Ferenczi saw clearly the ways in which psychoanalysis could be used to reinforce, to secure the difference between the generations, and how it could also be used to sabotage the mystique of that same generational difference. Psychoanalysis must be one of the last bastions of the spurious belief that wisdom necessarily comes with age (the most cursory contact with any respectable psychoanalytic training institution would quickly disabuse one of this). Psychoanalysis, as Freud's theory suggests, is everything to do with character and little to do with experience. Analysing a transference should spell the death of uncritical fantasies of expertise.

Ferenczi, Jones wrote in his biography of Freud,

had a bold imagination which readily carried him beyond the confines of the known. His honest and candid nature was such that he was extraordinarily prone to making slips of the tongue or other 'symptomatic actions' in a self-revealing fashion, which he would then gaily analyse in public. Among us he was called on this account the 'King of the Parapractics'.

Is a successfully analysed person – a good person, as it were – someone, like Ferenczi, 'extraordinarily prone to making slips of the tongue', or someone more like Freud who, by all accounts, made relatively few of the slips he gave his name to? Jones's short-lived paean of praise for his former analyst (he was to be only too ready to pathologize Ferenczi when he became 'difficult') confronts us with a question that goes to the heart of psychoanalysis and its history: is authority a capacity for making mistakes, or a will to concealment? In a profession whose moralism and claims to truth are rightly under suspicion, Ferenczi's lived life, and lived writing, offers us something too rare in psychoanalysis: the fluency of disorder, the inspirations of error. The spirit of psychoanalysis has not been resilient – but then, conviction often springs from the letter of the law. We need a new pantheon of bunglers. Psychoanalysis, at least, puts the slapstick back into our ideals.

Ferenczi exposed the defensive function of professionalism in psychoanalysis, and, by implication, the posturings of any professional identity unable to acknowledge (or enjoy) what it is organized to exclude. The reason, Ferenczi writes in his *Clinical Diary*, that he experimented with mutual analysis – being analysed, in turn, by his patients – was 'an awareness of an emotional resistance or, more accurately, of the obtuseness of the analyst'. Ferenczi, that is to say, was interested in the fact that he was frightened of his patients. Most psychoanalytic theory and technique conceals the simple fact that analysts are often frightened of their patients. By taking his own distinctive risks with psychoanalysis, Ferenczi was showing us that this was nothing to be ashamed of. Rather, it was a shame, and therefore worth thinking about.

2

Symptoms

I

What is the rule that says pain has a correlation?
Rachel Wetzsteon, *Parables of Flight*

People come for psychoanalysis – or choose someone to have a conversation with – when they find that they can no longer keep a secret. What was once private has become, in spite of oneself, unbearable; has become a means of recruitment, a message. A symptom is always the breaking of a confidence. Suffering, like desire, is the secret we may not be able to keep. Because it has the potential to rupture our fantasies of self-sufficiency, suffering can be longed for, and feared, as a medium for legitimate contact and exchange between people. Pain makes us believe that other people have something we need. When we suffer first, as children, we seek people out; and our wish to communicate, and our will to believe in comfort, is urgent. But as every parent – and every child – knows, what is being asked for is not always clear. The risk of having a need met – which confirms one's utter dependence (and potential envy of the person who can satisfy us) – is as great as the risk of misrecognition. If there is such a thing as help – a word which has always covered a multitude of sins, a word that is often the nice term for sado-masochism – it makes us wonder in what sense a need is something that can be known; what is it to want something (anything) from someone else? Because we can't help doing it, we can't help not noticing what we are doing.

Suffering, like desire, turns privacy into secrecy. From a psychoanalytic point of view a symptom is a (secret) way of asking for something (forbidden). This is what Freud meant when he wrote that the patient's symptoms *were* his sexual life. A symptom is the sign of a wish to make something known, but by disguising it – at

33

once a demand and an invitation. Or rather two demands: a demand to be accurately translated, or recognized – the wish that the object of one's desire gets the joke, realizes, say, that you keep blinking because you want to look at her; and a demand for satisfaction. Because desire is always, in part, constituted by the forbidden, every wish is ambivalent, its own best enemy. In this psychoanalytic picture we can't help but communicate, and we can't help but be baffled by each other. We always know too much and too little; we're always, in the words of the song, the first to know and the last to find out.

So Freud presented his patients – and his readers – with two useful paradoxes. Firstly, you can only tell yourself a secret by telling someone else. And secondly, people are only ever as mad (unintelligible) as other people are deaf (unable, or unwilling, to listen). It's not only beauty that is the beginning of terror, it's also listening. The psychoanalyst is paid not to talk too much, because talking is a good way of not listening. Being listened to – making one's presence felt through one's words, and through one's body which is making the words – at its best, restores one's appetite to talk. Symptoms – when the body takes over from the words – are a change of currency.

But what kind of expert, then, is the psychoanalyst? What, if anything, does he know that the patient or his family don't know? (Perhaps he is an expert on exchange rates.) If a family brings their child to see me, I can make available to them my knowledge of child development, my clinical experience of child and family therapy (informed by an array of theory), my willingness to listen, and my moral sense of how children and families should live. I might think of myself as something of an expert on children, or even on life. Or I might think of myself – mindful, in so far as I can be, of the potential for mystification, for covert seductions – as someone enabling the family to learn their own language. Attacks of panic, for example, look different when seen in the context of a trans-generational history of relationships to states of excitement in the family, compared to how they look from a psychoanalytic point of view. The psychoanalyst might assume that he is speaking a common language – call it, psychoanalytic interpretation – a form of Standard

English, whereas the family, like all families, has its own idiolect (think of family jokes). Psychoanalytic theory, in other words, is peculiarly adept at decontextualizing the lives it seems to explain (it is worth asking of any theory, What does it need to get rid of in order to work?). Psychoanalysts run the risk of believing that there is a King's English of the psyche and everybody is, or should be, speaking it. After all, why should everyone have to believe, or be assumed to *really* believe, that sexuality is an essential perplexity? (The fact that I can't imagine that it isn't is integral to the problem.) Who has met everyone? The analyst can be useful as someone who can say something at once odd and pertinent (which is what the patient does all the time without noticing). Hearing things that belong to the patient, he can suggest how they belong, which stories they could be part of. But psychoanalysts, like everyone else, have their favourite stories. The psychoanalysts who have come to believe them, or find them useful, learnt their relationship to stories – to doing things with words – in their own families.

The psychoanalyst, in other words, has a dilemma that the training institutions obscure by only teaching psychoanalytic texts (psychoanalysis, as Freud acknowledged, doesn't know anything that literature doesn't know). Either the psychoanalyst thinks he knows the best stories, and therefore should convince his patients of their viability; or, awake to the uses of fictions, he thinks of himself as an expert listener, someone who can bear and process what is called up in him when people talk about their urgent preoccupations and predicaments; someone who, by definition, traffics in the provisional and doesn't need to be believed; someone for whom coercing assent is always the problem (madness, Winnicott once said, is the need to be believed): someone unseduced by the idea that fanaticism is passion.

II

He must be distanced from the world if *he wants to get closer to it* . . .

Maurice Blanchot, *Adolphe, or the Misfortune of True Feelings*

In the light of all this I want to describe from what is, broadly speaking, an object-relations point of view, the relationship between the use and the meaning of a symptom: the eczema of a seven-year-old boy. This approach brings with it three questions, though others follow on from them. What kind of person does the patient use the symptom to construct as the recipient of its message? What kind of relationships does this entail? And what is the project of the symptom, what kind of world does it make?

Of course, psychosomatic symptoms such as this focus the familiar and far-reaching dilemma of what words can do to bodies. It is the psychoanalytic wish that words can lure bodies back to words; we don't, for example, tend to describe psychosomatic symptoms as simply other ways of thinking, but as failures of thought. (We could think of certain parts of the body – the skin, the genitals and the other orifices – as well suited to thinking specific things through.) But there is a virtual consensus, at least in psychoanalysis, that, as Nina Coltart has written, 'part of the mind has lodged on a psychotic island on the body . . . we have to ask what is the unthinkable content . . . How do we build a bridge which really holds over the secret area of the body-mind divide?' It is always worth wondering, as a prelude to a case-presentation such as this, what picture we have of what words can do to someone's body, of how they work inside him. And conversely, what bodily symptoms – the frenzy of a boy scratching his body – can do to our own words and bodies. Can one body stop another body thinking and saying specific things? Indeed, relationships are often sought out to make certain thoughts and feelings impossible (a symptom is always a rule by which the object must abide). Eczema gets under people's skin.

So I want to describe, in Winnicott's terms, the kind of environment – the 'nuisance-value' – the child's symptom created in the family and in the treatment – the way his scratching punctuated the conversation, and what kind of punctuation it was. (In retrospect I think 'orchestrate' may be more accurate than 'punctuate'.) So from this point of view the symptom is a mostly unconscious attempt – exploiting a somatic predisposition – to create a certain kind of environment. In cases of earliest onset we cannot easily say that this is their intention so much as their consequence; though by the logic of secondary gain – the pleasure accruing from the symptom that masks the pain that prompted it – consequences become part of intentions. I was told, for example, in the referral letter from the paediatrician that his mother complained that Tom scratched excessively with the result that more often than not she had to push him out of her bedroom and make him sleep in the living room. His symptom gets him to another place, and assumes a paternal function (it separates him from his mother, which is not only, of course, a paternal function); it was also significant, as I found out, that she had also made his father leave. Through his symptom he was in a double identification with his father: the father who prohibits the son access to the mother, and the father who is prohibited access to the mother. Rage, as we know, is often a solvent for confusion. But symptoms have a lot of psychic work to do.

The referral letter from the paediatrician told me the following. That Tom had first developed eczema as a toddler, and then again about six months before his father left, and he had had it ever since. Tom was being 'teased, bullied and sworn at at school, and was beginning to stop going to school, which, previous to the eczema, he had enjoyed'. His recent two-week hospitalization – in which his mother had not stayed with him – 'had an excellent effect, his skin was in extremely good condition and he seemed happier on discharge'. The paediatrician also mentioned that Tom's mother had asked him to support her request for rehousing because, in her view, 'the area is making him scratch'. Clearly both mother and son were trying to get away from – to evacuate – something experienced as debilitating. On arrival in hospital Tom had apparently been 'very tearful and said he felt his mother did not want him'. At every stage of separation – but not of rupture – this is both a wish and a fear. Of course the point at which the family requests something from outside the family is always revealing – as though it is assumed there is something the family itself does not have the resources to process.

In the first interview Tom came with his mother and his mother's mother. He was a neat and timid little boy with a slightly cheeky look on his face. Mother told me that Tom's eczema was much better but that they were all concerned with their poor housing conditions – they only had one bedroom, it was noisy, and above all the starlings 'kept banging at the window like they want to get in'. Once Mother started talking about the starlings Tom started frantically scratching his arms for the first time; up until then he had been, as I say, a rather demure, shy but composed little boy listening to his mother's story dutifully, as though it was an important lecture. He was, she told me, terrified of the starlings. I asked Tom if the starlings felt left out. He stopped scratching as though the question had concentrated him, and said, 'No . . . they're pretending . . . they like being outside really.' I said, 'Perhaps they are worried you'll forget about them?' And he agreed and started furiously scratching. I asked him if it was the question or his answer that made him scratch. He shrugged his shoulders despondently and said, 'The answer', and I suddenly felt a great pull of sadness. I said, 'Sometimes boys are worried that their mums will forget them and sometimes they wish their mums would forget them.' He giggled, as though I had told him a rude joke; at which point his mother, who had been listening attentively, intervened to say that Tom was not like a child, and that, just as her mother was her best friend, she was Tom's best friend. I asked what Tom would have to do when he wanted to be treated like a child. She replied by telling me that she wondered whether his eczema was a way of 'getting attention'; that there were times when she was talking to friends, and particularly to her boyfriend, when he would feel left out and start scratching. (When people are described as attention-seeking – attention is a good thing to be in search of – it is always worth wondering what, in themselves, needs attending to.) I asked what it felt like he was saying when he did this and she said that he 'needed her'. I wondered whether this sometimes suited her and she grinned in agreement.

I suggested that they might both be in a muddle; they weren't sure whether they wanted to be together all the time or apart all the time. Tom once again began scratching, and said in a hushed tone, 'Together, together.' I suggested that the eczema made her look at him, but made her unable to do anything for him . . . but before I could finish my little lecture she interrupted with a kind of relish of disgust, 'But it's revolting!' Prompted by something, I immediately asked how Tom's dad fitted into the picture. And Mother said in a sad, defeated, bitter kind of voice that his dad was a 'revolting' man who she had had to 'kick out' two years ago. I asked what was revolting about him – at which point Tom started scratching – and Mother said she didn't want to say. I wondered whether Tom was holding on to his father by making himself revolting. Tom, coming to life, stopped scratching and shouted 'No!' and told me his dad was a pig and he never thought about him and never would. I said that perhaps everyone in the family felt that they had to agree that his dad was a bad man. This was greeted with a dead silence; there was a great deal of anxiety in the room and quite quickly we found ourselves talking about their housing problem.

I did, of course, take this seriously, and on their own terms. I told them I regretted that I could do nothing about their housing, and therefore that what I could do for them was limited. But once everyone's defences had settled down, I asked by way of conclusion – noticing that Tom was tired and had had enough – whether anyone else had eczema in the family, at which point Grandmother told me the story of Mother's eczema: she had been a very clingy child who had got eczema just before puberty. Not surprisingly, this story woke Tom up a bit, though I understood that he had heard it before on several occasions. I asked Mother how she had got rid of it. And she said, with some pleasure, 'I cured myself when I realized I wanted to show people my arms.' I said, 'When you wanted other people, apart from the family, to be interested in you?' She agreed with this and then she and her mother told me, with a good deal of affection, what a 'wild girl' she had been as an adolescent. So I said, 'Perhaps in your family when people feel tempted to explore the world outside the family they get eczema?' This clearly interested all of them, and Tom was manifestly calmer. I said that I thought they had all been doing a lot of work looking after each other but perhaps we needed to understand what it was that they needed to protect each other from. (People in families look after each other with their symptoms.) We agreed to have one more family meeting with a view to offering Tom individual psychotherapy.

They arrived promptly for the next session and began by saying that Tom's eczema was continuing to improve. After this there was a pause and Mother said that there was something that she ought to tell me that our last session had 'made her think about'; indeed she had been 'depressed' last week and could hardly think of anything else. This confession was in fact the history of her early relationship with Tom. She told me that Tom was not a premature baby but had spent the first few weeks of his life in an incubator. His mother, who was very young (fifteen) and felt 'very inexperienced', was left alone in the maternity ward, 'the only mother without a baby'. After this terrible separation she had not been eager to hold Tom; it was as though, she said, they had 'missed a stage'. She had never felt properly close to him and once she took him home her mother did most of the looking after. She still lived with her mother; her father had left just before she got pregnant and the father of her child lived nearby with his parents. He was clearly involved with and loved his son, but the couple's relationship was always stormy. It sounded as though Mother had brought Tom home, given him to her mother – by whom he had been very well loved – and in considerable confusion and distress resumed her 'wild' adolescence. It was a palpably desolate story. I said, 'So you and Tom have had to find a way of getting to know each other?' She agreed and said that Tom had first begun to get eczema when he was a toddler and began to 'love danger'. She described several incidents of Tom wandering off when she was shopping or exploring things he knew were dangerous like electric sockets. Once he started taking risks and getting eczema, she 'couldn't stop thinking about him'. I said, 'It sounds like you lost him when he was born and then when he started getting lost you found him again; but finding him released so much love in you that he needed to protect himself a bit with eczema.' This clearly made sense to her and she said, 'Yes, it's like armour.' Throughout all this Tom had been drawing a house on the floor and listening intently. This seemed to be the main work of the session.

When Tom had discovered new bits of independence and autonomy in himself his mother had started to bond with him as though he were a new baby. But then his mother's delayed – or deferred – finding of Tom made what felt like an overwhelming demand on him. His eczemetic 'armour' functioned as a particular kind of boundary between them at a time when Tom would have been waking up to three-person relationships. But like all symptoms, from a psychoanalytic perspective, it was profoundly over-determined (symptoms are opportunists: they do all the work they can). His mother's extreme concern mobilized a self-protective rage that was turned against himself. At each new stage of fresh curiosity about the world Tom got eczema partly, perhaps, to reassure his mother that the world was a dangerous place and therefore he needed her and could not do without her, at a time when she might be, as she was after his birth, feeling depleted and redundant. The eczema mobilizes her love and concern but sets – or repeats – the limits of her capacity to modify his pain. It is interesting that when people have eczema they don't invite someone else to scratch it for them.

But it is also important to remember that at a later date Tom had actually witnessed his mother rejecting a man; she had, as the family story went, 'kicked out' his father, soon after he had moved in with them, because he was 'revolting'. And Mother was unable to speak the full provenance of this crucial word (at least to me). We can, therefore, reconstruct a possible, unavoidably tentative story. We can imagine Tom perhaps registering a very early experience of discontinuity – of being 'dropped' in Winnicott's language – but this was mostly compensated for by the hospital and his grandmother, who constituted a sufficient holding environment, to which Mother was some kind of adjunct. But he is nevertheless left with what we must call, for want of a better language, a 'memory-trace' that equates separation and independence with rupture. Somewhere in himself he believes (which is also the wrong word) to an excessive degree that he can neither be contained nor contain himself in his own skin. So risks are taken, almost compulsively, to test the environment, the environment of his skin and the world beyond his skin. Both to find out if they are different, and to find out who or what is there for him and what they are like. For example, can he be torn up by his own rage? How does the immediate environment read his eczema, what kind of invitation does his family experience it as? What makes them disappear and what do they return for? And he can, retrospectively, give meaning to this early rupture by transposing the separation of his parents back on to it – reading a pre-Oedipal experience Oedipally (which may be all anyone ever does anyway).

For Tom, at an Oedipal level if men are rejected because they are revolting, then in order to be a man (like your father) you have to be revolting; if you are revolting, your mother rejects you. By the unconscious logic of identification, this must then suggest to the child that what is revolting about him is his maleness. It will, I hope, be obvious by now that Tom was in a very complicated predicament. At the very end of what was an upsetting session, I said that Tom was wondering what kind of man he wanted to be. And for the first time in the session he began to scratch himself again, albeit quite gently. I suggested that, though Tom was obviously doing well – his skin was much improved, he was enjoying being back at school, and he had a new best friend – we should meet for a few individual sessions; to which Tom was very agreeable.

I would like, by way of conclusion, to say something about the first session of individual psychotherapy. We met six times and the therapy consolidated the work begun by the 'crisis' hospitalization. Broadly speaking, imaginative elaboration of the father made rage against the mother (and the father) more tolerable. It was as though Tom, once he could allow himself to stop propping up Mother's version of his father, acquired more confidence in Mother's resilience, her capacity to metabolize the intensity of his feelings. He became, in Mother's words, 'more impossible', less compliant as his eczema cleared up. And during the six weeks in which I was seeing him, Mother found a boyfriend, and moved out of her mother's house to live with a friend.

When Tom arrived for the first session he went eagerly to the drawing materials and started drawing a 'knight in armour'; I remembered with him that his mother had described his eczema as armour. He ignored this and went on drawing, very absorbed. We sat in silence for about twenty minutes while he did this and I was struck that he was drawing armour at the same time as making me feel that I would be violating his concentration if I was to start talking. We were definitely there together; there was a boundary between us but not an obstacle.

On completing this striking drawing, he stared at it as though he were looking in the mirror, with a kind of intense, blank curiosity. I asked him what happens when the knight takes his armour off. He said, 'People come and see him . . . and they bark.' I said, 'That sounds like a dream,' and he told me he once had a dream in which a man took off his armour and dogs – 'which he thought were his friends' – came up and bit him. I said, 'That sounds frightening,' and he replied, 'No, because I woke up.' I said, 'You can't eat if you don't bite,' and he smiled and made growling lion noises. I said, 'Perhaps when you scratch you're scratching those hungry dogs?' He said, 'Yes, and stop talking.' He then started looking round the room, as though for something else to do, and said, 'Have you got any glue?' I said, 'Yes, I think so.' And he said, becoming whimsical in a light-hearted way I hadn't seen before, 'I think so, I think so,' in a kind of half-mocking imitation of me, then he paused and said, 'What's thinking?' I said, 'What is it for you?' and he replied very intently, 'I asked first!' I said, 'It's trying to remember what you want.' And he said, 'I want to fly' – he said it with all the relish of imagined potency. It seems, in retrospect, an interesting transition: a demand for glue, through a question about thinking, which intrigued and surprised me, to a wish to fly.

III

When we make life difficult for our parents, he said, we make
something of ourselves.

Thomas Bernhard, *Gathering Evidence*

If a child has a fantasy that his mother controls his body, or a fantasy
that she doesn't, it may be reassuring to find a symptom like
eczema, that continually informs you about the limits of your
mother's words: they do not stop the scratching. Since most children
suffer from an excess of attributed meaning from parents and other
adults (including analysts), an unreachable psychosomatic
symptom can be a paradoxical area of privacy: a part of the self that
defies intrusion while keeping you in contact with the people you
need. And this fits, I think, with what is, developmentally, a central
paradox for the child (though its repetition during adolescence is
often more vivid): a good-enough environment can only be constituted by putting it at risk (like a good-enough theory). A
psychosomatic symptom like eczema tests the integrity of the body
and the family. A skin is a place in which and through which risks
can be taken. The child, every so often – at points of growth – has to
test the environment; one might say, after Anzieu's description of
'the skin ego', the child has to test the skin of the self and the family
in the quest for resilience and permeability. 'It is a healthy thing',
Winnicott writes, 'for a baby to get to know the full extent of his
rage . . . if a baby cries in a state of rage and feels as if he has
destroyed everyone and everything, and yet the people round him
remain calm and unhurt, this experience greatly strengthens his
ability to see what he feels to be true is not necessarily real.' If one of
the aims of psychoanalysis is to increase the repertoire of possibilities for exchange – to enable the patient to forget himself, to freely
associate – then we have to work out for each symptom (which is
always over-determined; it has more than one purpose, serves many
masters), and for each individual (whose complexity always eludes
us, and him), which forms of exchange are being averted. And what
is the catastrophe that these forms of exchange seem to invite? Or,

to put it another way, one is always analysing how a person organizes their life around a sense of entitlement: the titles given, that is to say, to the entitled self (greedy, selfish, ruthless, generous, arrogant, anarchic, dependent, envious, promising, inspired, etc.). However painful or pleasurable themselves, symptoms are always a self-cure for terror and ecstasy, ways of dosing the intensity of what people feel for, and want from, each other. Realizing, as psychoanalysis does, that symptoms are a form of cure – local anaesthetics, as it were – might make us wonder what kind of symptom the cure of psychoanalysis is. The aim of psychoanalysis, after all, is not to cure people of their conflicts but to find ways of living them more keenly.

Writing of William James's pragmatism, Frank Lentricchia suggests that James is always asking, in his writing, 'Does the world rise or fall in value when any particular belief is let loose in the world?' This is the question the patient is asking with his symptoms – which are always beliefs, states of conviction about the self – and that we should ask of the theories that come to meet them. It is not that the analyst must abrogate his theories – how could he? – but he must assume they also have a defensive function. He must be alert to what exactly he uses them not to hear. The risk of psychoanalytic theories, of psychoanalytic expertise, is that it won't even meet the patient half-way. The psychoanalyst may think he is better off being more interested in psychoanalysis than in other people. Psychoanalysis, at least, is something one can specialize in.

3
Fears

How am I supposed to acquire evidence for the universal hoax?
Anthony Kenny, *Faith and Reason*

There is a Sufi story that Idries Shah tells – though there are versions of it, I think, in other cultures – in which Mulla Nasrudin is standing one morning in the yard outside his house throwing corn. A man who is passing stops and looks at him, extremely puzzled. 'Mulla Nasrudin,' he asks, 'why are you throwing this corn around?' 'Because it keeps the tigers away,' the Mulla replies. 'But there aren't any tigers here.' 'Well, it works then, doesn't it?' the mulla says. I want to appropriate this as my first psychoanalytic parable about fear. The story raises a number of questions: had there actually been tigers in Mulla Nasrudin's life that he had warded off with corn, or was this more like a symbolic ritual passed down through the generations, an integral part of a larger cosmology? Was there once a threat of tigers in the mulla's life, and did he then dream up this idea of the corn which, coincidentally, worked – he threw the corn and the tigers never came back, and he deduced his system accordingly?

Clearly, a story like this, rather like a joke, is meant to avert this kind of tedious consideration; like the corn, it just works. The story makes it surprisingly difficult for us to think that the mulla is wrong, or ridiculous, or deluded. The joke might be on us if we assume that kind of superior or enlightened position. The story ends up making you wonder how much of your life is spent throwing corn, and perhaps what your own, personal tigers are. Like the man who stopped to ask the mulla what he was doing, we may end up being rather relieved that someone else is throwing the corn for us, so we don't even have to think of the tigers. The mulla himself is clearly determined not to forget them. Throwing the corn is a way of keeping them in mind.

I want to limit the resonance of this story – that is, to interpret it – by using it to say something about the psychoanalytic idea of defences, or defence-mechanisms, as they are sometimes called to convey something of their automatic or compulsive nature (the fact that they tend to operate unconsciously). The ego's defences are both prompted by fear, and used to regulate it; they are the ways in which the organism prevents itself from being overwhelmed by stimuli. We have to imagine that the ego (perhaps unconsciously) already knows what the tigers are, what they represent – whatever it is we fear and believe we cannot manage (though we might, as the philosopher Sartre does, want to know where it gets this knowledge from). And we have to assume the ego – call it Mulla Nasrudin – already has rigorous moral-cum-aesthetic criteria to rely on, though it may 'know' that a tiger is bad before it can allow itself to know exactly what a tiger is (the defensive ego has a kind of pre-emptive morality born of fear, it prejudges in order not to judge, in order not to have to think too much). What the story of the mulla tells us, in these terms, is that fear, like desire, tells us very little about its object. You cannot get from corn to tigers without an explanation. Our forms of self-protection don't necessarily or obviously tell us anything about what we are protecting ourselves from, or what we are frightened of. Because of this, interpretation is required. We need to explain the mulla's explanation. Indeed the definition of a primitive defence (like Klein's concept of splitting) is that it creates the illusion that the object of fear was never there in the first place; in this sense *we* can also use corn to protect us from tigers in Britain.

Unlike the mulla's corn, certain defences not only protect us from the supposed object of fear, but also from the knowledge that there is such an object. But what does the way we construct our defences – repression, splitting, projective identification, denial, etc. – tell us about what we fear? Common sense would tell us that we can infer the enemy from the armour; that fear is self-defeating if it is not accurate as to its object (though Auden's question, 'Is a shield a weapon?' complicates this). The story of the mulla tells us that fear can be a threshold – a kind of transitional state – between knowledge and superstition. The mulla's corn-throwing proves conclusively either that tigers are terrified of corn, or that there are, in fact, no tigers there; this is the kind of suspension of disbelief, the comforting uncertainty, that can make such defences so effective. The mulla is keeping the possibility of tigers, of dangerous excitement, in the picture; his defence keeps the possibility of tigers alive.

From a psychoanalytic point of view, the way we construct our defences tends to suggest that we unconsciously invite, or sustain contact with, whatever we fear. Throwing corn becomes a way of thinking about tigers. (In the same way sadness, for example, can be a way of reminding ourselves of what's missing in our lives.) By constructing fear as a form of desire, by redescribing it as a particular kind of excitement, psychoanalysis has made the object of fear – the place where the fear is located, the tigers – a paradox: both elusive and irresistible. Like its new-found twin, the object of desire, we can't find it and we can't get away from it. As in a neurosis, we are pursuing something by running away from it. (The neurotic is always arriving at the place he is running away from.) Once every fear is a wish, as psychoanalysis asserts, our fears become the clue to our desires; aversiveness always conceals a lure. Fear, like its accomplices, disgust and shame, is psychic work; it's something we make. What may feel like a reflex may have an elaborate invisible history. Fear, as Freud shows, is both a recognition of pleasure (and/or pain) in the offing, and a form of secret pleasure in itself. People don't tend to boast about their fears, perhaps because they are sometimes superstitious about losing them.

What psychoanalysis can show us, within the language game of its own vocabulary, is that fear, far from being exclusively a reflex, a natural reaction, is also constructed. And, more specifically, that fear is constructed through the ways we protect ourselves from it. The over-protected child wonders – fantasizes – what is out there that he needs so much protection from ('Best safety lies in fear', Laertes says to Ophelia, trying to out-tantalize Hamlet with an old pun). Another way of saying this is that psychoanalysis can show us, from developmental theory and reconstruction, how we construct our fears (like precious artefacts), but it cannot always show us, though it usually wants to, what it is that we are really frightened of. What it can do, at its worst, is persuade someone of the source or object of their fears. In this sense there are two kinds of psychoanalysis: one helps the patient to locate his fears, and then to live accordingly; and one shows the patient what he uses his fear to do – what kind of instrument it is. (Our relationship to our fear contains within it our unconscious picture of fear as an object.) It is the difference between a psychoanalysis intent on finding the enemy – like Kleinianism, for example, with its horrified devotion to the death instinct – and a psychoanalysis that is committed to conflict without, paradoxically, needing the idea of an enemy. It is, of course, a fundamental form of tyranny to coercively ascribe a fear to someone (or to coercively describe a person, or a part of a person, as unequivocally bad). All forms of salvation, all the redemptions, depend upon a consensus about what there is to fear.

Psychoanalysis, in all of its versions, is a story about what there is to fear; like the symptoms it can sometimes explain, it is grounded in terror. The instincts, desire, aphinisis, the death instinct, castration, impingement, separation, the experience of being dropped, intrinsic prematurity, inauthenticity, gender trouble, the violence of the imaginary – all these, and there are more, provide the foundation for psychoanalytic theory and practice. However much psychoanalysis aspires to be non-essentialist, the stories it cannot help telling about human development are rife with intimidation. Development is trauma, and trauma in its various forms is the subject-matter, the material of psychoanalysis. And, by the same token, each version of psychoanalysis sponsors a different form of hope (which may itself turn into a tyrannical demand). But can a theory based on fear do more than endlessly repeat itself when it takes fear as its subject? Can it, as it were, seperate the tigers from the corn, or does it just have to go on throwing its corn, despite the fact it doesn't always work? What kind of future is fear – or psychoanalysis as a pheno-menology of fear – preparing us for?

II

*Fear won't always save you, but it will take some of the pressure
off your luck.*

Tobias Wolff, *In Pharaoh's Army*

If fear is a form of anticipation, of hope inverted, then to talk about
fear is to talk about our fantasies of the future and of our relationship
to these fantasies. The target of our fear – even if its putative source
is in the past – is whatever might happen next that will involve, in
that felicitous word, unpleasure (the negation of well-being).
Grounded in terror, Freud sees the human subject developing in
something akin to a war situation – not so much open combat as the
more insidious and uneasy truces of protection rackets. Describing
the infant's first fear in *An Outline of Psychoanalysis* (1938), Freud
constructs a mafia-like scenario:

the weak and immature ego of the first period of childhood is per-
manently damaged by the stresses put upon it in its efforts to fend off
the dangers that are peculiar to that period of life. Children are protected
against the dangers that threaten them from the external world by the
solicitude of their parents; they pay for this security by a fear of loss of
love which would deliver them over helpless to the dangers of the
external world.

The dangers of that period, in Freud's view, are the internal dangers
arising from the instincts, and the more obvious threat of an
inhospitable world. Life is made viable by the protection of our
parents. And the kind of viability created by their protection
becomes something of a blueprint for later life. As Freud writes in
one of his last published notes (June 16, 1938), 'in connection with
early experiences, as contrasted with later experiences, all the
various reactions to them survive'. The way Freud puts his point
about the legacy that this earliest parental care entails is of interest.
Children, he writes, 'pay for this security by a fear of loss of love
which would deliver them over helpless to the dangers of the
external world'. Clearly we are not to assume that the parents extort
this fear as the cost of their protection; but this originary and

constitutive fear – of loss of love – is a payment; there is an exchange, an intra-psychic deal going on. Parents give you something that you then fear losing, their love. If you want a future, you must suffer a fear for it, for its possible loss. This fear of loss of love is both the cost of the future, and what keeps the future alive. This fear is the costly consequence of the infant's somatic acknowledgement of a truth: the infant is not self-sufficient. In this deal that Freud is describing, the child, in some ways, registers the helplessness that comes with a life; and then, as his side of the bargain, pays himself and his parents back with this constitutive fear of loss of love. This fundamental (quasi-Faustian) pact is then repeated, with significant modification, in all the child's later developmental crises: weaning, castration anxiety, primal scene fantasies are echoes of this pact, confirmations of insufficiency. Being 'delivered over helpless' – a virtual description of the human from Freud's point of view – is the catastrophe that parental love is meant to avert. Children, one could say, are loved into a belief that life is worth living – partly because every adult has a doubt about this (and then, some children can feel morally obliged, as it were, to sustain their parents' hope). Life is usually stronger than people's love for it.

For Freud, this first helplessness, which is, in his view, both the source of the individual's fear and its target, becomes a powerful explanatory device – a simple insight that was itself to be the source of much more sophisticated and elaborate theory. 'The relation of the child's helplessness to the helplessness of the adult which continues it', he writes in *The Future of an Illusion* (1927), '(are) the motives for the formation of religion.' Fear was the founder of religions, as of neuroses (people are not bad, they are frightened). Fear is clearly linked in Freud's writing with dependence, and the related question of agency; fear becomes both a recognition of its absence, and a relative limitation: our fantasies of autonomy are circumscribed by fear. But fear also initiates the child into the question of agency. The evolving question for the infant and child is: What capacity do I have to secure a future? All the child's initial resources are in the service of sustaining parental co-operation (Freud assumes, of course, that there is a sense in which the child wishes to have a future). Every successful action, or pleasurable experience, felt to be initiated by the child brings with it the possibility of its loss. Each increment of future life, each achieved pleasure, has a price; the presence of satisfaction carries with it the terror of its future absence. Every gift is a possible future theft. Fear constructs disappearing acts; it attempts to save the disappearances. 'Children are protected against the dangers that threaten them from the external world by the solicitude of their parents; they pay for this security by a fear of loss of love which would deliver them over helpless to the dangers of the external world'. Fear, in its first scenario – or first Freudian scenario – is a truth-telling, the way in which absence announces itself to the individual, the absence which can destroy the future (every suicide dispels the tyranny of hope). The fear that is not overwhelming (or paralysing) is a prompt or a goad to action; born of fear, individuals do what they can to redeem the absences, to recuperate the future. They make demands. They try to secure the love that is already contaminated by its potential loss. Fear, in this sense, becomes the matrix for, the ground of, the ego's illusion of agency, the impossibility of a mastery that will always elude it. The kind of paradoxical mastery represented by the Mulla Nasrudin: corn for tigers.

Reactive to fear – at first, the fear of loss of love – the individual is projected into a future committed to curing the absences, all the time undermined by the constitutive truth captured in that fear – fear betokens our insufficiency: it points to what is missing. From a common-sense point of view, fear of loss of love instigates a project to secure that love. From a psychoanalytic point of view, the implication of Freud's description is more paradoxical. Fear of loss of love instigates a project to secure something that by definition cannot be secured. Fear becomes the perception of a truth that inspires tenacious denial. In that formative Freudian fear we acknowledge that the future cannot be guaranteed; and then we set out to guarantee it. Fear discloses an ineluctable potential for loss; and so it confronts the child with desire as contradiction, the to and fro of emptiness and plenitude; with emptiness always defined by the shape that will fill it. Fear is the cost, what the child pays for this recognition that inaugurates his project. Fear inspires futures that it has already perceived to be instrinsically uncertain. In fear, and perhaps out of fear, we make a future we also cannot afford to believe in. Only megalomaniacs make promises.

Fear, as I have been suggesting, is a state of mind in which the object of knowledge is the future, but it is, of course, a knowledge that can only be derived from the past. Whether it is literally from birth, as Rank proposed and Freud partially endorsed, or from later experience, there is a backdrop of loss and privation to this insistent anticipatory knowledge. In Freud's simple account of fear, which will also become a theory of anxiety, it is a state of mind that is the site of an epistemological conflict – a conflict experienced and repeated in the pain of unmet demand. In the original fear of loss of love we have to imagine that the child is poised between (or straddles) epistemological conviction from the past – the certainty that presence is shadowed by absence – which is also a form of profound scepticism – the terrifying uncertainty generated by the fact that presence is shadowed by absence. The child 'knows' both things, both the certainty and the uncertainty. That is to say, the child's experience of desire or need provides him with paradoxical knowledge that the future is not definite. (In this context belief in repetition is a form of hope and children, of course, are passionate about repetition). What the child is saying, in Freud's account, in what he calls 'the to and fro between disavowal and acknowledge-ment', is this: what I want is what makes wanting impossible; what I know is what makes knowing impossible. Getting what you need has the fear of losing it built into it; as an experience from the past and, therefore, as a possibility in the future. The cost of wanting is the terror of losing – of not securing for the future – what you have received. This is what we know in fear.

The future that is known, or surmised, in states of fear is a repertoire of possibilities from the past. The object of fear is a future set in the past. In fear the imagined future joins up with the unpleasure of the past. Tell me what you fear and I will tell you what has happened to you. But by the same token, the knowledge born of fear closes down the future. Knowing what you fear is a way of living in the past. By throwing corn, Mulla Nasrudin may be keeping the tigers away, but he is also warding off the future, the future he has no way of thinking about except in terms of tigers. The tigers guarantee a predictable future.

III

New truth is always a go-between, a smoother-over of transitions.

William James, Pragmatism

For my second parable about fear I want to modify a story Sartre reports hearing from Janet, and which he uses to illustrate, in *The Transcendence of the Ego*, what he calls a 'vertigo of possibility'. We might call this, more blandly, a fear of freedom, just to make ourselves wonder why we attach fear to certain versions of freedom – what fear is doing there. If boredom is one of the ways we break our habit of believing in the future, then fear is one of the ways we keep the future going.

In this story a young and newly married couple come downstairs each morning and have breakfast together. Then the wife helps her husband on with his coat, and waves him off to work. The young woman then spends the entire day sitting by the window crying until her husband returns. This perhaps dated and rather arch tale creates an interesting interpretative dilemma. A conventional quasi-psychoanalytic interpretation of this woman's behaviour might suggest that she was suffering from a separation anxiety – perhaps an echo of more troubling separations in the past. After all, when her husband returns, she feels better. Psychoanalysis, that is to say, shows the patient that she is living as if something were true: as if, for example, free time was sexual time, or as if sexual partners are really the police. An existentialist interpretation would see this as a theory compounding, being of a piece with, the real problem. To talk here about separation anxiety and the distant past is merely complicitous – as much bad faith as the woman's 'symptom' – because when this woman's husband leaves her in the morning she can, within certain constraints, do what she wants. She has turned her fear of freedom into a form of grief. If she is mourning anything, it is the loss of her guardian, who psychically has become a kind of prison warder, or at least an especially attentive parent. Once her husband leaves, she is confronted with the question: What does she want to use her time for, what is she going to do? And the answer, given her fear, is that she is going to do nothing – or rather, she is going to cry and wait for her husband's return. She is going to start missing, and looking forward to, the return of the past. But in this interpretation, which too easily disparages the woman, what does her fear consist of? If she didn't have it, as a kind of substitute for her husband, what would she be doing? What is she using a husband, and, by implication, other relationships, to protect herself from?

The only accurate answers to these questions would, of course, be the ones that she herself gave. Without those, we are in the interesting position of having to imagine and attribute fears to her, on her behalf, so to speak. Freedom, of course, is not a psychoanalytic term; fear of freedom is not an idea that is easily compatible with most psychoanalytic theory. So what do we have to confer on this woman, or put into the idea of freedom to make it frightening? What does freedom have to be, or seem to contain, in order to scare us off? In Sartre's view, it is possibility itself; in this situation the woman is unavoidably confronted by herself as someone with a capacity to make choices. What Sartre puts into the picture is agency. The idea of agency means that there is nobody (no God or anyone else), and no other 'things' (instincts, the putative past) controlling one's life. It is, then, something about the solitary nature of a life – a life as fundamentally unsanctioned or simply beyond legitimation – that in Sartre's account frightens this woman. Her symptoms are not so much an expression of her fear, as the way she has evolved of concealing her fear from herself. Fear, in this context, is potentially the route to authenticity. It would be like the medium of contact through which this woman could rescue herself from (Sartre's) bad faith. The aim of an existential analysis would be to introduce her to her fear and what it portends for her. What this otherwise anti-pathetic view shares with a psychoanalytic account is a belief that fear signifies proximity to something of value, perhaps of ultimate value. And so, by implication, the belief that there is something about what we most value, or about what is most integral to our lives, that frightens us. Fear becomes a guarantor of validity. Whether it be instinctual life, the vagaries of our past desire, or the unknowable future that our choices precipitate us into, fear, in its very disarray, orientates us.

So is fear a form of knowledge, or intelligence – an acute recognition; is there a sense in which we always know what there is to fear? Or does fear signify the breakdown of these capacities. Does fear start as cognition breaks down? In Sartre's example are we to assume, as a psychoanalyst might, that the woman knows, however unconsciously, what she wants to do with her so-called freedom, but because it is forbidden she cries off? Or is the fear exactly the opposite: that at the moment her husband leaves she enters an unknown and unknowable future? In other words, a determinism, like psychoanalysis, gives fear an object (castration, say, or the unprotected past); without a ghost in the machine, without an essential cause, as in Sartre's existentialism, fear loses its grip; its object, if it can be called an object, becomes an empty category (the unknowable, or the future). Where we locate the fear, and, secondarily, how we go about doing so, tells us a good deal about who we think we are. For Sartre, 'I know what I fear' is a contradiction in terms; for Freud, it is, because of the unconscious, an absolute truth. So instead of asking, Is there an unconscious?, we might ask, In what sense are our lives better if we live as though there is one?

For Freud, fear returns us to what we already know; it is a symptom of knowledge, knowledge of and from the past. The uncanny, as he said, is where we feel at home. For Sartre, fear points us in the direction of the unknown. It cannot return anything to us, it can only lead us away from our supposedly familiar selves. For Sartre, fear is the shock of the new; for Freud it is the shock of the old, it is elegiac. If, for Freud, fear is knowledge – knowledge disguised as shock, concealed in excitement – and for Sartre fear indicates its absence, what, if any, family resemblance is there in their distinctive uses of this term? Certainly for both of them fear is a message – a reaction to a plenitude or an absence of resources – and they articulate their own projects by deciphering it. And for both of them fear is an ironic form of self-protection – for Freud self-protection from the past and for Sartre (absurdly) self-protection from the future. The potential paralysis of fear is also a kind of royal road to those things for which they have the highest regard: a certain kind of self-knowledge or a certain kind of impossibility of self-knowledge. For Sartre, fear is refusal of the self-knowledge that tells you your future selves are unknowable; they cannot be predicted, they can only be performed. They are constituted by choice, not inflicted by some prior agency called the past, or instincts, or the unconscious. For Freud, fear is our acknowledgement, however disguised, of the past: an involuntary self-knowledge. For Freud, self-knowledge can only be knowledge of past selves, which, for Sartre, is precisely what renders *self*-knowledge absurd. For Sartre, knowing oneself is a form of bad faith.

If the young wife in Sartre's story goes out when her husband leaves, what will become of her? Who might she turn into? For Sartre, the point of the fear is that she does not and could not know. Her fear stops an unknown future from happening: she uses it as an obstacle. For Freud's Little Hans – another person frightened to go out – psychoanalysis seemed to confirm that his fear (or phobia, in psychoanalytic language) was an attempt to stop a known future from happening again. Of course from Sartre's point of view the theory of repetition itself could be another piece of bad faith, an especially suitable alibi. Indeed this misgiving might make us wonder, as we look at the case of Little Hans, what fear, or so-called self-knowledge, would be like if we did not believe in repetition? If there was no such thing as repetition, what would we be using fear to explain? If there was no repetition – if we stopped believing in such a thing – what self would we have knowledge of?

IV

*I really do think that the crowning glory of the Sex Pistols is that
we've always managed to disappoint on big occasions. When the
chips were down, we never came through.*

Johnny Rotten, Interview

Repetition is reassuring because it implies that there is a recognizable something – a pattern of relationship, a scenario, an impulse, a
fear – that is being repeated. Repetition confirms our powers of
recognition, our competence at distinguishing the familiar from the
unfamiliar. The repetitions in our lives are like our personal
collection of secure referents. The knowledge that is fear, or the
knowledge fear protects us from, is born of recurrence, or its
possibility. Once unpleasure has been experienced its anticipated
repetition has to be pre-empted. It is interesting, I think, how often
the frightening experience and its possible repetition are dealt with
by a complementary form of repetition. Both the mulla and Sartre's
young wife, faced with the tigers and the husband's absence
respectively, evolve a kind of ritual to manage their fear. They do the
same thing each morning; they enact a reliability, a predictability
they know to be precarious – a certainty the future cannot guarantee.
They behave as if they know what they are frightened of; if they did
not believe they knew this, there would be no solution available:
their fear is an act of faith. It has to have – or has to construct – a
relatively stable referent, otherwise the ritual solution would be felt
to be hopelessly ineffectual. If it was tigers and possibly elephants
and possibly wolves, the mulla would be all over the place.

In the light of Freud's descriptions, we can imagine a process: the
child has an experience of unpleasure, which is then assumed to be
repeatable; fear is the recognition of unpleasure as potential repetition. But if this assumption of repetition is viable, we must identify
what there is to fear, what it is that might return – loss of love, say, or
hunger or the cold. So in fear we assume the future will be like the
past; and we believe – that is, behave as if – we know what that past
was like. Fear, in other words, makes us too clever; or at least

misleadingly knowing. Knowing becomes rather literally the process of jumping to conclusions. In fear the wish for prediction is immediately gratified; it is as though the certainty – the future – has already happened.

'A face which inspires fear or delight (the object of fear or delight)', Wittgenstein wrote in the *Philosophical Investigations*, 'is not on that account its cause, but – one might say – its target.' Freud, like Wittgenstein here from a quite different perspective, is raising a simple question: does fear have an object or only a location? (Do we know what we are frightened of?) Does the fear already exist, waiting to be evoked, or inspired, repeatedly waiting to be placed? We could say, for example, that fear does not have a cause, but fear makes us want to ascribe causes. Perhaps the most difficult thing to acknowledge, to bear, is that there is a feeling called fear that has neither a cause nor an object. Certainly fear, at least from one psychoanalytic point of view, makes us want to believe in causality (in cure). Given the infant's helplessness, given instinctual life and its critical culmination (or consummation) in the Oedipus complex, fear has its definable causes. And yet with the concept of anxiety, as used in the case of Little Hans, the question, Does fear have an object or only a location? is provisionally complicated.

Psychoanalysis has tended to answer this question with an assertion – a simple distinction – that has the kind of clarity that psychoanalysis itself has made us question. Fear, in the words of the early British analyst John Rickman, 'is occasioned by a real object, [anxiety] is characterized by an indefinite feeling of expectation about something but lacks an object'. So one of the aims of psychoanalysis is to turn anxiety back into fear, to locate the object that the ego uses anxiety to conceal from itself. Fear is the real thing – which implies a human subject secure in its capacity for knowledge; anxiety is a terrible scepticism, an unknowing full of ominous expectation. Fear has an object, anxiety has a vague location. Anxiety is a defence against fear, a refusal to know what we are frightened of.

Fear, in Freud's description of its earliest stages, is a process of jumping to conclusions, a potentially misleading form of anticipatory knowledge in the service of self-protection – fear as the potentially false belief that the future will be like the past. And here Rickman, along Freudian lines, offers us fear as acknowledgement of reality, and anxiety as a defence against reality. In its 'indefinite feeling of expectation' perhaps Rickman's anxiety is both like and unlike what Freud called the child's fear of loss of love. It is fear, in that it has a real object – the child's experience of loss of love – and it turns into anxiety if it takes the form of a perpetual unease derived from that fear but not consciously linked with it. Anxiety in this model is the way a person hides something from himself. But this fear 'occasioned by a real object' can lead someone to fantastic conclusions; can turn into anxiety. In psychoanalytic terms fear is always the first state of anxiety. So-called fear of loss of love might turn, say, into an anxiety about finishing a piece of work because it involves separating from it. But it will be obvious, also, that this distinction between fear and anxiety – between having a referent, and reference being itself what is in question – aligns psychoanalytic practice with instrumental reason. We must locate our fears and act accordingly. As though at least at the beginning of the story we know where/who we are, then out of fear we mystify our knowledge.

Little Hans, a boy of five treated by his father under Freud's supervision, was frightened that a horse would bite him in the street, and so was frightened of going out. 'Hans's anxiety', Freud writes in this bizarre case history, 'which thus corresponded to a repressed erotic longing was, like every infantile anxiety, without an object to begin with; it was still anxiety not yet fear.' The aim of the defensive infantile ego was to turn fear into anxiety, to detach fear from its object. The aim of psychoanalytic interpretation is to turn anxiety into fear, to find its object. There is something rational and intelligible and interpretable called fear that has a referent; there is something irrational, unrealistic, like a fear of being bitten by a horse, called anxiety that is elusive. An original and fundamental intelligibility that is unacceptable, too painful, is concealed by something vagrant, intent on concealing its real identity. 'When once a state of anxiety establishes itself', Freud writes, 'the anxiety swallows up all other feelings . . . all affects are capable of being changed into anxiety.' Anxiety is a successful defence because it makes discrimination impossible; in fear we have the clarity of true knowledge. It should be noted that Freud is using the idea of fear here to describe a human subject that is fundamentally realistic – intelligibile to itself – but driven by fear into the self-obfuscation of anxiety. In the case of Little Hans, which, Freud insists, confirms directly his earlier theories about infantile sexuality, we are given a version of 'neurotic' development as the transformation of 'realistic' fears of abandonment and castration into irrational anxieties.

Through Little Hans's strenuous psychic work, the horse, Freud writes, 'was being exalted into the object of his anxiety'. The making of the phobia, that is to say, was an act of devoted idealization. 'The essence of Hans's illness', Freud writes, 'was entirely dependent upon the nature of the instinctual components that had to be repulsed . . . The content of his phobia was such as to impose a very great measure of restriction upon his freedom of movement, and that was its purpose. It was therefore a powerful reaction against the obscure impulses to movement which were essentially directed against his mother.' By turning his fear into anxiety, Hans, in one sense, gets what he wants: by being frightened to go out, by being troubled, he gets more care from his mother; and he becomes, as the case history shows, a central preoccupation of his father. He restores something of his place in the family before his sister was born. But from Freud's point of view, Hans's anxiety gives him back a past; his fear gives him a future. His anxiety – and this is part of his underlying intention – keeps him in the family and keeps alive an impossible project: sexual relations with his parents. His fear of castration, according to the logic of the theory, forces him to move on towards genuinely available objects. His fear involves him acknowledging a loss – the hopelessness of an erotic life with his parents – which opens up future possibilities; his anxiety keeps him in suspended animation. The function of anxiety is to sever the future from the past; the function of fear – of fear as a version of realism – is to make an unknowable future out of the past.

There is a convincing logic to this; but I think the very clarity of the distinction Freud uses to organize his case history has a doubt built into it. We see Hans confronted by at least two immensely powerful adults: Freud and his father. Hans has anxieties and Freud has knowledge of fears. In Hans's father's postscript to the case, he reports that, 'a trace of his disorder still persists . . . only in that of the normal instinct for asking questions'. 'Once when he had tired me out with his questions', Hans's father writes ingenuously, 'and I had said to him, "Do you think I can answer every question you ask?" he replied, "Well, I thought that as you knew that about the horse, you'd know this too." ' Presumably, in this system, if you can translate anxieties into fears, you must know everything. 'An unsolved residue remains behind', Hans's father writes, 'for Hans keeps cudgelling his brains to discover what a father has to do with his child, since it is the mother who brings it into the world.' In the few, usually patronizing, glimpses in the case history of Hans's mother, she is seen taking Hans at his word, not translating him. Hans's question, What has a father to do with his child? can be answered in the context of the case history: the father is the one who tells the child what he fears; he is the one who knows the difference between an anxiety and a fear. Hans's profound question is also, of course, a question about his father's relationship to Freud.

Freud's distinction between anxiety and fear instates a difference it appears to reveal; and it is a difference that psychoanalysis depended on. Is fear realistic, as Freud insists, or is the concept of fear an attempt to assert, to foist on us, a concept of the real? Or, to put it another way: is fear the truth about anxiety, or is anxiety the truth about fear? Is the analyst supplying persuasive referents – abandonment, instincts, incestuous desire, castration – and turning anxieties back into their sponsoring fears; or is he loosening the existing referents – the most addictive ones – releasing fears into anxieties? Does fear have a cause or only a target? In psychoanalysis can we find what we are frightened of – something that the analyst can have prior knowledge of – or can we only map the vagrancy of our fears? Freud's authority, like all authority, is constituted by his knowing what people are frightened of; by providing the most persuasive account of our fears (by stressing the significance of childhood experience, for example, psychoanalysis has made adults frightened of children). Like Little Hans, we have to assent to this repertoire of fears; without this assent, psychoanalysis has nothing to offer us.

4
Dreams

Anyone who sleeps sleeps heroically
Keith Waldrop, 'Lullaby in January'

Freud's description of the unconscious shows us new ways of keeping secrets, and a new rationale for doing so. A dream is enigmatic – it invites interpretation, intrigues us – because it has transformed something unacceptable, through what Freud calls the dream-work, into something puzzling. It is assumed that the unacceptable is something, once the dream has been interpreted, that we are able to recognize and understand. And this is because it belongs to us; we are playing hide-and-seek, but only with ourselves. In the dream the forbidden may become merely eccentric or dazzlingly banal; but only the familiar is ever in disguise. The interpreter, paradoxically – the expert on dreams – is in search of the ordinary. There are, Freud writes in his essay 'On Dreams', 'certain experiences which one cannot escape in analysing dreams':

I should come upon dream-thoughts which required to be kept secret in the case of *every* dream with an obscure or confused content. If, however, I were to continue the analysis on my own account, without any reference to other people (whom, indeed, an experience so personal as my dream cannot possibly have been intended to reach), I should eventually arrive at thoughts which should surprise me, whose presence in me I was unaware of, which were not only *alien* but also *disagreeable* to me, and which I should therefore feel inclined to dispute energetically, although the chain of thoughts running through the analysis insisted upon them remorselessly; and that is to suppose that these thoughts really were present in my mind . . . but that they were in a peculiar psychological situation, as a consequence of which they *could not become conscious* to me . . . Thus we are led to the concept of a 'dream-distortion', which is the product of the dream-work and serves the purpose of dissimulation, that is, of disguise.

Freud's method of interpretation reveals that, in actuality, no thoughts are alien: they are only made alien *because* they are disagreeable. And, more paradoxically, that only I can be an expert on myself; in fact, I am already an expert, but I work at being a stranger. I dissimulate because I am an expert on what I cannot bear. The dream reveals the sense in which we translate ourselves: and the irony of the fact that we are the translators. It is like pretending not to be a double agent, by being a triple agent instead.

Freud's assumption, placed in parenthesis, that nothing as personal as the contents of a dream could possibly be addressed to another person – could be, in any sense, for human consumption – is also ironic in these circumstances. His insistence is that the message of the dream has to be kept from someone: if not oneself, then certainly other people (as though the personal *is*, in some sense, the forbidden, the indecent; and privacy is secrecy). But if the intensely personal is not really alien to oneself, why need it be alien to other people? And if Freud is determinedly disqualifying dreams as currency between people – as 'intended' only for oneself – where does this leave the practising psychoanalyst?

If Freud is intimating here that we should keep ourselves to ourselves – that psychoanalysis is something to do on your own – he is also complicating the idea of the psychoanalyst as expert. In so far as we are unacceptable to ourselves – which requires at least two versions of ourselves, the Censor and the Dissident – we have to make secrets of ourselves (we have to find ways of telling ourselves lies). And the first secret might have to be that there are these two versions, so we behave as though we more or less know who we are (we don't like the sound of hearing voices because we usually pretend to know where voices come from). It is as though we have to render our desires, our perceptions, our histories, opaque – or at least above suspicion. But in Freud's view, we are turning something essentially familiar – something obvious and ordinary and known in some sense – into something bizarre. Something we may need an expert, or perhaps only a method, to disclose. 'The task of the therapist', Freud writes, in 'Psychoanalysis and the Establishment of the Facts in Legal Proceedings', 'is the same as that of the examining magistrate. We have to uncover the hidden psychic material; and in order to do this we have invented a number of detective devices, some of which it seems you gentleman of the law are now about to copy from us.' But in Freud's view, we are at once the criminal, the detective and the crime.

Dreams, Freud intimates, are evidence of something. But evidence of something so dismaying, so shameful, so terrifying, that it must not be shared. As he wrote, 'an experience so personal as my dream cannot possibly have been intended to reach' anyone else; a dream is like a letter without a signature or an address (a blackmail that the victim mustn't know about?). Freud's use of the word 'possibly' as over-emphasis here is, of course, suggestive of other possibilities. But we may still feel fortunate that this terrible message can at least be hidden in something as ridiculous and obscure as a dream.

The dream contains something that can be understood and communicated to another person, but it mustn't be. Freud makes us wonder what the worst things are that we could say to other people. (Relationships are often constituted by what one dare not say to the other person.) And yet in 1895, a long time before he wrote 'On Dreams', Freud had written to his friend and collaborator Fleiss: 'Do you really believe that some day on this house one will read on a marble tablet: "Here revealed itself, on 24 July 1895, the secret of the dream to Dr. Sigm. Freud"?' If the dream contains something so shameful, then to crack the code of one's own dreams is to be the ultimate hero of one's most personal truth; to understand dreams *per se*, the dreams of others, may be perilously close to a violation, to overexposure. After all, as Freud had discovered, dreams exist in the first place because people don't want to know what they know. The only legitimate rationale for revealing the truth of dreams was that people suffered from their simulated ignorance. The truth cannot save us, Freud knew – indeed psychoanalysis makes a mockery of the redemptions – but ignorance can exacerbate our misery. We work hard to keep our terrors, if only as punishment. The dream – a unique source of personal news, Freud believed – offers us a choice: how can we include dreams in our lives (other than by dreaming them – they include us whether we like it or not), and why would we want to? Similar questions, of course, can be asked of our sexuality. But then to talk about dreams, for Freud, *was* to talk about our sexuality. Perhaps that, too, is an experience so personal that it cannot possibly have been intended to reach someone else? Freud shows us, in other words, how intimacy makes us unsociable; especially the intimacy we have with ourselves.

II

Each one is Tantalus to what he dreams . . .
Charles Madge, *Delusions II*

There is a famous parable by Kafka called 'Leopards in the Temple' whose title immediately makes you wonder what they could be doing there. The title could be a statement, a question, or a cry of alarm (as is often the case with Kafka's titles). The parable itself is simply one sentence:

Leopards break into the temple and drink to the dregs what is in the sacrificial pitchers; this is repeated over and over again; finally, it can be calculated in advance, and it becomes part of the ceremony.

We have to assume that what was once a violation becomes a transformation. We don't know from Kafka whether the leopards in the temple enrich the ceremony or simply become something the ceremony has to accommodate. But something unpredictable, something as anomalous as leopards in the temple can now be calculated in advance and even included. So what happens to something like dreaming (or sexuality, in words) when it becomes part of a ritual like psychoanalysis? I want to use this parable to say something about two different but related processes: the eruption of dreams into psychic life, usually at night; and the intrusion and inclusion of dreams into a kind of conversation called psychoanalysis. In each context – the intrapsychic and the interpsychic – the dream breaks in, like the leopards, and participates in a repeated ritual: the ritual of sleep and the ritual of analysis. The question is, What are we doing when we include dreaming in a context other than sleeping, where, after all, we have no choice? It is not only the ceremony that is changed by the inclusion of the leopards; we also begin to see the leopards differently once we calculate upon their participation. Leopards in the temple, leopards as part of the ceremony, are very different from the creatures we couldn't possibly imagine inside any building, let alone a temple. The dream-like parable, deliberately exempt from psychological explanation, makes us wonder: Are the leopards incorporated in the ceremony out of terror (the people making a virtue of necessity and complying), or out of resignation, (the people taking the line of least resistance), or out of wonder (the people being provoked into fortuitous discoveries)? In the terms of my reading of this parable, the question is: In what kind of spirit do analysts include dreams in their therapeutic ceremonies? And, perhaps more importantly, in what spirit do their patients include them? From the analyst's point of view, the leopards are already in the temple; from the patient's, they aren't, or they are part of a different ceremony, or the patient knows that to be in the analyst's ceremony dreams are required.

It is easy, I think, for therapists embroiled in their trainings, or their institutions, or their larger professional worlds, to forget this question of context. If I make a Freudian slip in a group of psychoanalysts, it has a quite different significance to a slip made when I am preaching a sermon or ordering newspapers over the phone. In a group of psychoanalysts my slip may be a piece of unconscious mockery, a wish to make the group cohere in its amused and shared recognition, or a reassuring confirmation of a shared belief system. 'The use of dreams in analysis', Freud wrote, 'is something very remote from their original aim.' This significant remark assumes either that Freud knows their original aim or that he has an intimation that the use of dreams in analysis is different from some other use that is more important. At its most minimal, this remark reminds us of two things: we do *use* dreams in analysis; and dreams might have an aim or purpose that has nothing to do with analysis, or indeed with self-knowledge.

The analyst, that is to say, has a very specific relationship to dreams, which is both difficult to define and likely to be very different from the patient's, at least initially. I would imagine that very few analysts ask their patients for their theory of dreams – what they believe dreams are, what their function is and what kind of relationship they have to them. To enter analysis, of whatever persuasion, is to be initiated into, or persuaded to believe ('At the end of reasons', Wittgenstein wrote, 'comes persuasion'), that dreams have a very specific purpose in one's life (secular oracles, say). By definition the analyst is likely to have a far more elaborate and articulated set of beliefs about dreams than the patient. At the outset of the treatment what the analyst might want from the patient's dreams, and what the patient might want (if anything) may be quite different – why should they be the same? When the leopards break into the temple, who decides – who is in a position to decide – how they should join the ceremony? 'The use of dreams in analysis is something very remote from their original aim.' This implies that dreams have their aims built into them, not that their aims are constructed by us. There is no reason to believe, from a psychoanalytic point of view, that our beliefs about dreams are any less wishful than our dreams themselves.

This is a roundabout way of saying something simple, but which has complicated consequences: in so far as the patient accepts the use of dreams in analysis, he may have complied with something – he has accepted the ceremony, leopards and all. From the analyst's point of view, this might be called 'allowing the process'; from the patient's point of view, it might be experienced as accommodating or submitting to something. From the child's point of view, shit can be wonderful and yet it gets thrown away. The child might have all sorts of other ideas about what could be done with it, but ultimately there's nothing else for it: it has to go. Shit, *unlike* some other bodily products such as dreams, is of limited use; whatever the child's repertoire of interpretations of it, broadly speaking only one thing happens to it. However imaginative or permissive the parents, the child (and the parents) submit to the parents' interpretation: shit is something you dispense with.

Paradoxically this is the paradigm, I think, for certain elements of the analytic ceremony (the parent decides). It is not that the patient is obliged to accept the analyst's interpretations of his dreams. But rather, prior to that, he is obliged to accept that dreams can be interpreted in a certain way, and that they have a certain functional relationship to more conscious waking life – whether it be as the disguised fulfilment of repressed wishes, the return of the unacceptable, a processing of emotional life that is another way of thinking, or whatever. The risk is that the patient's idiosyncratic relationship to his own dreams is subsumed by the analyst's therapeutic relationship to the dream. After all, the patient is an experienced dreamer. I think it extremely unlikely that, aside from the available clichés in the culture about dreams, the patient won't have his own theory about dreams, his own use of them. Not only has the patient noticed – if he is not too frightened, or too uncurious – that leopards break into the temple most nights, that there are strange goings-on in his mind that are called dreams, he has also grown up in a family or environment from which he has learned, implicitly or explicitly, theories about dreams. The child notices that dreams are told or not told, responded to in certain ways and not others, perhaps talked about as a subject or referred to in snippets of conversation. Somebody, for example, says that something was 'like a dream' and the child might wonder, What is it for something to be like a dream? Or even, What is a dream like? The dream, that is to say, has existed as a peculiar object in the environment and in the self – like and radically unlike other objects – over a long period of time (if we take dreams as the norm, for example, then language can begin to seem surreal). And the child has an evolving relationship with the idea of the dream and with the dreaming experience itself – with how dreams punctuate or sometimes rupture the apparent continuity of psychic life – every child has had a nightmare and so knows, somewhere in himself, what dreams can do – and with how dreams fit, even by their absence, into ordinary conversation.

After all, dreams are a very odd way of speaking (they don't come in sentences, they are silent); we may understand all the words in the description, but the scene described is often very bizarre (like leopards in a temple). By entering therapy, the adult, who has been this child, enters a conversation in which the dream and its associations, though still bizarre, are an integral part of the conversation, and for some analysts the virtual precondition for a distinctively psychoanalytic dialogue. Here, at least to some extent, the dream fits, even fits in. But there is no reason to believe that everything in a life – each thought, feeling, action, dream – can be linked, or must fit in. It is the making coherent of a life – the forcing of a pattern — that people often suffer from (symptoms are ways of willing coherence). I want to stress how peculiar it is for someone to make that transition, from leopards breaking into the temple, to leopards becoming part of a ceremony. For the therapist this has already happened; for the patient, however knowledgeable about analysis, it only happens when the patient begins the treatment. When the patient enters treatment, the leopards have already broken into the temple, but a ceremony is about to begin with them. Out of the dream, and the ceremony of its interpretation, a fundamental question arises that is integral to the nature of the treatment: Who's ceremony is this, and who decides? And these questions generate further questions: What is the use of these dreams? What happens to, or is the function of, the uninterpreted dream or the unreported one? Who knows what these dreams of mine are for turns into the question, Who's dreams are they, who do they really belong to? Dream interpretation – so obviously essential, so taken for granted in analytic practice – becomes the site for a crisis of appropriation. I am often surprised how easily, indeed keenly, patients take to working with dreams; so I have also found it useful to listen out for their resistance not only to interpretation, but also to the process of interpretation itself. According to the theory, in our dreams we are, however disguised, at our least compliant; in our use of dreams in analysis we can be at our most compliant. The therapist can be compliant in his unquestioning acceptance and use of the available theory; and the patient can comply by bringing dreams, and submitting them for interpretation.

III

People are much more eccentric than they are supposed to be.
Randall Jarrell, *Pictures from an Institution*

In relation to this complicated issue – what kind of currency are dreams, or have they become, in analysis? – there has been a shift of emphasis in some current thinking about dreams. Masud Khan and J.-B. Pontalis, both wary of the way in which the interpretation can usurp or steal the dream, want to return us, in theory, to the patient's experience of the dream, rather than to its meaning. The role of the analyst is then to help re-evoke, to elicit, the lived experience of the dream – its affective content – rather than to translate it into a substitute parallel text, one supposedly more authoritative than the manifest content of the dream. The analyst, encouraging description of the dream, is in effect asking the patient (and himself) not, What does it mean? – What are the latent dream thoughts? – but, What was it like to be there? What was the patient using that unique space to do? The dream becomes the place of – or the psychic space for – different versions of self-experience, a setting for other voices. The dream becomes an evocative object as opposed to an informative one. (They are not, necessarily, mutually exclusive.) Protecting the patient's dream from the analyst's interpreting machine – the analyst's influencing machine – runs the risk of idealizing the idiosyncracy of the dreamer. And by contrasting meaning and experience – the dream as informative object versus the dream as evocative object – Khan and Pontalis sometimes imply that there is a real thing called experience that falls into meaning; that interpretation is corruption. In fact, a good interpretation is not true, it is just more or less interesting, more or less prolific in its consequences. But what Pontalis and Khan are doing, I think, in their papers 'The Use and Abuse of Dream in Psychic Experience' and 'Dream as Object', is trying to locate what cannot be stolen from the patient – what, in the dream, is beyond appropriation. The meaning of a dream can be competed for; the experience of the dream can't. We may speak in words, but we don't dream in them.

IV

Tired of the old descriptions of the world . . .
Wallace Stevens, *The Latest Freed Man*

Psychoanalysis is a conceptual apparatus that invites the leopards into the temple, and makes them integral to the ceremony. But as I have been suggesting, the question, Who are we dreaming for? is bound up with the question, What kind of object is a dream for us? What do we want to use dreams to do for us? As Freud shows in *The Interpretation of Dreams* – and this is as essential to his argument as his own discoveries – people have answered these questions in different ways, at different times and in different cultures. The dream, and its uses, have a history. If we tend to want dreams to tell us secrets (about the past, about desire), if we treat the dream as our internal double-agent (the artist as spy), we also have to remember that this has not always been the case, and need not be in the future. Each of us is involved in situating ourselves in relation to the dream – a relationship that has both a personal and a cultural history, and an unknowable future. What will the dream be for us tomorrow?

Is dream interpretation something we learn, once and for all, like swimming, and then go on doing more or less well, but without significant innovation (as psychoanalytic theory would suggest)? After all, there is a limit to what one can do in any medium. But what kind of limits does the dream as an object seem to impose; what are the constraints on our use of a dream, and who could be in a position to decide them? To ask what kind of object is a dream is to ask, What do we think of a dream as being like? Or, In what sense is an ordinary conversation less perplexing than a dream? Do we think of the dream as more like a film, a prophecy or a rebus? Who we are dreaming for, how we imagine this, will depend on the kind of answers we find ourselves giving to these questions. In an important footnote added to the 1914 edition of *The Interpretation of Dreams* Freud wrote, 'It has long been the habit to regard dreams as identical with their manifest content; but we must now beware equally of the mistake of confusing dreams with latent dream-thoughts.' Freud is trying to work out something very puzzling here: What is the dream identical to? If it is not the same as the manifest content or the latent dream-thoughts, what, then, can it be equated to? What kind of object is the dream? How can we know when we've got to it? What Freud, I think, was committed to was the dream as the elusive object, as the paradigm for the ungraspable, an invitation to make meaning that we can never fully accept. (Dreams are not like machines; they do not come with people who know how they work.) The dream is always more than, other than, what we can find to say about it; and in this sense it confronts us with the ways in which we are never identical with ourselves. To say that we dream is to say that we do not know what is going on inside us, we don't understand the language that is going on. But, by the same token, we go on comparing it, finding likenesses – likenesses that are *not* the dream, but what we might call aspects of it. Interpretations are more or less persuasive aspects, ways of keeping the story going, ways of moving the dream on. The interpreter is never sufficiently competent: the dream cannot be exhausted. The dream is whatever we can find to say about it; and whatever seems to be left out by what we have said. In any interpretation there is always a remainder of possibility. The material does not submit. At its most minimal, the dream is a new description of the world; the new as the bewildering.

Dreams can be used in different ways. For example, in Pontalis's words, they can be used to represent 'experience or as a refusal of experiences', interpsychically (between people), and intrapsychically (despite Freud's misgivings). They can be used in as many ways as we can think to use them. But if the uses of the dream are various, there is a consensus about one aspect of the dream: it is a communication, a message of whatever sort. We use the dream – or rather, the dream uses us – to speak; to whom and about what is contentious. But we can use this contention as a repertoire of internal voices or points of view. Indeed, to take seriously the idea of over-determination is to assume that the dream is dreamt for a multiplicity of purposes. In so far as this dream is a message to the analyst, what is being said? In so far as it is a message to the patient, what is being said? From a false-self point of view, what is the message? What is the homosexual self using this dream to do? And so on. The dream becomes the product of an always contentious collaboration of different parts of the self. Condensation, displacement, considerations of representation – what Freud describes as the dream-work – are all ways of incorporating what might be called an excess of points of view (the dream-work, as Freud said in another important footnote, is *the meaning of the dream*). The dream itself, in so far as it has not become a nightmare, has apparently, and temporarily, conciliated rival internal claims. And the unacceptable, in this context, is the point of view that must not be considered. If we are Freudians, we might think of these as points of view from childhood, disguised representations of infantile sexuality; if we are Kleinians, we may be thinking of something more 'primitive'. As Freudians, we have to think of the dream as deeply nostalgic; as post-Freudians, perhaps we should also think of the dream as a psychic sample of our irreducible complexity. And our contemporary dilemmas about the dream perhaps reflect this. Our conceptual systems – Freudian, Kleinian, Jungian, etc. – are like containers for our inner complication, for the multiplicity of dissenting voices – a kind of exercise in damage limitation. The leopards break into the temple and we make them part of the ceremony, but it doesn't stop there. It isn't only leopards that we have to contend with. There are the creatures we know about, and the ones we have never heard of. And none of our ceremonies lasts for ever.

'If we consider the dream as an object', Pontalis writes, 'and as intimately related to the object of nostalgia . . . then it does not give rise to a single relation, but to a number of "directions for use", and it does not have the same function for each person.' If it is possible, as Pontalis asserts, that dreaming does not have the same function for each person, then how are we to include this in our ceremony? What would psychoanalysis become – be like – if we were to attend not only to the patient's personal dream idiom, but also to the idiosyncratic function of his dreaming? We would no longer only be asking: What do this patient's dreams mean? But, What does *this particular person* use dreaming for, use dreaming to do?

The dream is not the only object of nostalgia; we may also be nostalgic about – or even unable to mourn – our interpretative procedures. If we are, in Quentin Skinner's words, 'challenging and replacing descriptions instead of attempting to enhance them', our theories about dreams might become as bizarre, as ample, as our dreams are. Our methods of interpretation can be used to protect us from the dream, but also to protect us from each individual's interpretation of dreams. Who is the expert on the dream and of what, exactly, does his authority consist? The dream, Freud implies, makes a mockery of its interpreters. Dreams are there to be dreamt. But once another person listens to them, all sorts of things can happen; a psychoanalyst may be no more and no less than a person one tells one's dreams to, a person one knows to be interested in such things. If dreaming does not have the same function for each person, though, our methods of interpreting dreams are put into question. The leopards are different and so is the ceremony.

5
Sexes

I

To speak of Narcissus is to speak
of conviction . . .
Stephen Dunn, *'Wanting to Get Closer'*

If, as Freud suggests in *The Ego and the Id*, character is constituted by identification – the ego likening itself to what it once loved – then character is close to caricature, an imitation of an imitation. Like the artists Plato wanted to ban, we are making copies of copies, but unlike Plato's artists, we have no original, only an infinite succession of likenesses to someone who, to all intents and purposes, does not exist. Freud's notion of character is a parody of a Platonic work of art; his theory of character formation through identification makes a mockery of character as in any way substantive. The ego is always dressing up for somewhere to go (the poet Jane Miller refers to identity as a 'posture of status'). In so far as being is being like, there can be no place for 'true' selves or core gender identities. After all, my sense of authenticity can only come from the senses of authenticity in my culture. In this context my 'true self' is more accurately described as my 'preferred self' (or selves). I am the performer of my conscious and unconscious preferences.

Lacan's mirror-stage is a testament to the havoc wreaked by mimetic forms of development; and Mikkel Borch-Jacobsen and Leo Bersani, in particular, have exposed the violence and tautology of Freud's theory of identification, the mutual implication and complicity involved in being like. This critical concept of identification is the nexus for a number of contentious issues: it invites us to wonder what we use other people for, and how other they are. In fact it forces us to confront the question that excercised Freud and which object-relations and relational psychoanalysis take for granted: in what sense do we have what we prefer to call relationships with each other? And, perhaps more importantly, how do we go about deciding – or who is in a position to decide – what a relationship is? How do you know if you are not having one?

In the *Three Essays on the Theory of Sexuality* Freud proposed that the object was merely 'soldered' on to the instinct, that our primary commitment was to our desire and not to its target. He was implying that we are not attached to each other in the ways we like to think. In this book, as in *The Interpretation of Dreams* Freud glimpsed the ego's potential for promiscuous mobility. Dreams, in particular, revealed that psychic life was astonishingly mobile and adventurous, even if lived life was not (very few people are actively bisexual yet everyone is psychically bisexual). Freud had to explain this disparity – the fact that we don't have the courage, as it were, of our primary process – and also find a way, in theory, of grounding the Faustian ego, defining its loyalties when they sometimes seemed unreliable. The ego certainly seemed shifty in its allegiances, and so it was with some relief that Freud turned to mourning, which seemed to reveal that the ego was grounded in its relationship with loved and hated others. Mourning is immensely reassuring because it convinces us of something we might otherwise easily doubt: our attachment to others. The protracted painfulness of mourning confirms something that psychoanalysis had put into question: how intransigently devoted we are to the people we love and hate. Despite the evidence of our dreams, our capacity for infinite substitution is meagre. In this sense mourning has been a ballast for the more radical possibilities of psychoanalysis. It is the rock, so to speak, on which Prometheus founders.

It might at first seem more accurate to say that for Freud it was the Oedipus complex that both constituted and set limits to the exorbitance of the ego. But it is, as Melanie Klein has shown, the mourning entailed in the so-called resolution of the Oedipus complex that consolidates the ego. Without mourning for primary objects, there is no way out of the magic circle of the family. Indeed, partly through the work of Klein, mourning has provided the foundation for development in most versions of psychoanalysis; so much so, in fact, that mourning has acquired the status of a quasi-religious concept in psychoanalysis. Analysts believe in mourning; if a patient was to claim, as Emerson once did, that mourning was 'shallow', he or she would be considered to be 'out of touch' with something or other. It is as though a capacity for mourning, with all that it implies, constitutes the human community. We can no more imagine a world without bereavement than we can imagine a world without punishment.

Certainly mourning can sometimes feel like a punishment for our attachments; and from the outside, when one is not, apparently, grieving oneself, it can seem like a waste of time, and like the waste that time inevitably is (what, for example, is the evolutionary value of mourning?). The stubborn fact of loss, its unspeakableness, sets limits to invention, even if the prodigality of loss in any life, and the necessity of our own death, also prompts our resources. Our ingenuity lies in turning losses into gains, which Oedipus did and Narcissus couldn't (it is possible to be undaunted by impossibility). The good life, in psychoanalysis, seems to involve a talent for giving things up, but with no guarantee of satisfactory replacements. The pragmatist might want to ask – as indeed Freud does in *Mourning and Melancholia* – a seemingly callous, or even nonsensical question: how can we make mourning work for us? Or, how do we, because our resilience itself can seem demonic? (Man, Dostoevsky famously remarked, is the animal that can adapt himself to anything.) How can we link loss to the sense of possibility that our lives depend upon? How can loss keep us kind?

Somewhat along these lines, Judith Butler, in her radical essay 'Melancholy Gender/Refused Identification', is trying to use mourning to give some gravity, in both senses, to her exhilarating notion of gender as performative, as constructed self-invention. What is remarkable about her essay is that she manages to do this without the argument degenerating into the more coercive pieties that talk about grief usually brings in its wake. Mourning makes moralists of us all. There are only ever going to be as many gender identities as we can invent and perform. So we should not be celebrating those people, many of whom are psychoanalysts, who, in the name of truth, or psychic health, or maturity, seek to limit the repertoire. We know how many sexes there are, but we will never know how many gender identities we are capable of.

It is now a cliché, in theory if not in practice, that all versions of gender identity are conflictual and therefore problematic. What Butler is proposing with her notion of a melancholic identification, a 'culture of gender melancholy in which masculinity and femininity emerge as the traces of an ungrieved and ungrievable love', is a new version of an old question about gender identity. Why are homosexual attachments – the inappropriately named 'negative' Oedipus complex – described aversively, even if not originally experienced as such? Why are these manifestly passionate loves disavowed, made unmournable, repudiated and then punished when witnessed in others? At its most minimal, it seems clear that the culturally pervasive hostility – both inter- and intrapsychically – to homosexuality is based on envy (contempt is always disowned shame). If some heterosexuals in pre-AIDS times were explicitly envious of the promiscuity of homosexuals – Why can't *we* cruise? – heterosexuals now may be more likely to envy simply the intimacy some people are free to indulge in and elaborate with people of the same sex. But if, as Butler suggests, 'masculinity' and 'femininity' are formed and consolidated through identifications which are composed in part of disavowed grief, what would it be to live in a world that acknowledged and sanctioned such grief, that allowed us the full course of our bereavement of disowned or renounced gender identities? What would have to happen in the so-called psychoanalytic community, and in the wider community, for an ethos to be created in which people were encouraged to mourn the loss of all their repressed gender identities (or to consider their resurrection)? These are questions of considerable interest, providing they don't entail the idealization of mourning – its use as a spurious redemptive practice – as a kind of ersatz cure for repression, or the anguishes of uncertainty (to love mourning is to fear excitement). The convinced heterosexual man can become, in Butler's words, 'subject to a double disavowal, a never having loved and a never having lost' the homosexual attachment; is it, then, to become integral to the psychoanalytic

or engineer the undoing of, this disavowal, even if
nan claims to be relatively untroubled by it? The
le logic of Butler's argument poses some telling
Who, for example, ultimately decides what
m for the patient? And by what criteria? Assumed
every bit as much of a 'problem' as any other
(all symptoms, after all, are states of fraught
Certainly it's worth remembering the cost, the deprivation, involved in all gender identities, not to mention the terror
informing these desperate measures. 'There is', Butler writes, 'no
necessary reason for identification to oppose desire, or for desire to
be fuelled through repudiation.' But there is, of course, a necessary
reason given a certain kind of psychoanalytic logic. In Freud's view,
we become what we cannot have, and desire (and punish) what we
are compelled to disown. But why are these choices – why can't we do
both and something else as well? – and why are they *the* choices?

These were the issues opened up in Judith Butler's book *Gender
Trouble*. The essentially performative, constructed nature of gender
identity makes all constraints of the repertoire seem factitious and
unnecessarily oppressive. But just as every performance is subsid-
ized by an inhibition elsewhere, so there is no identity, however
compelling the performance, without suffering. If the idea of performance frees identity into states of (sometimes willed) possibility,
mourning refers those same identities back to their unconscious
histories, with their repetitions and their waste – those parameters
that seemingly thwart our options. Mourning and performance –
and the performances that constitute our sense of mourning – seem
usefully twinned. Without the idea of performance, mourning
becomes literalized as truth – our deepest act; without the idea of
mourning, performance becomes an excessive demand – pretend
there's no unconscious, then pretend what you like. 'I believe in all
sincerity', Valéry wrote, 'that if each man were not able to live a
number of lives beside his own, he would not be able to live his own
life.' Valéry's ironic sincerity – from which of his lives is he
speaking? – invites us to multiply our versions of self as some kind of
psychic necessity, as though we might not be able to bear the loss of

not doing so. But how many lives can the analyst recognize in, or demand of, his patient, and what are the constraints on this recognition that so easily becomes a demand? The repertoire of possible selves can only come from the culture, and yet the gene-pool, so to speak, of available identities keeps mutating, keeps being added to. The psychoanalytic situation seems potentially a good place for the speaking of new selves. But how does the analyst distinguish – in herself and in the patient – between a new self and a resistance (or a problem)? Especially as the new often begins as a pretence or a fear.

II

(Of course, I now see that good behaviour is the proper posture of the weak, of children.)
Jamaica Kincaid, *A Small Place*

In analysis, of course, it is not only the patient's gender identities that are at stake. Both the analyst and her patient are working to sustain their desire, and desire depends upon difference. There always has to be something else, something sufficiently (or apparently) other. The spectre of Aphinisis, Ernest Jones's repressed concept of the death of desire, haunts the process. But though desire depends upon difference, we only like the differences we like ('Why is difference always linked with hatred?' Coleridge asks in his Notebooks, making us wonder how that link is made); the set of desirable or tolerable differences, desire-sustaining difference, is never infinite for anyone. Psychoanalysis is about where we draw these constitutive lines.

Any clinician is only too conscious of the unconscious constraints on possibility that are called symptoms (and from a different perspective are called the Oedipus complex). But of course what is possible in analysis, or anywhere else, is dictated by the analyst's theoretical paradigms, by the languages she chooses to speak about her practice. Despite boasts to the contrary – psychoanalysis, the Impossible Profession, etc. – psychoanalysis is never more difficult than we make it. For example, from a clinical point of view, Judith Butler's initial political voluntarism in *Gender Trouble* would have made analysts wary. But there is no obvious reason why analysts in their practice have to be less imaginative than Butler is asking them to be. The analyst who believes in the unconscious can hardly set herself up as a representative of the authentic life, though the language she uses to talk about her job is full of the jargon of authenticity (integrity, honesty, trust, truth, self, instinct, etc.). The language of performance may be too easy to dismiss clinically as evasive in a way that is blind to the theatricality of the analytic situation (in a psychoanalysis the audience is merely invisible). The concept of identification puts the notion of the performative back into the analytic frame; what is more surprising is the way we can use mourning as a way of nuancing the theatricality that is integral to our making of identities, our making ourselves up through loss (our capacity for sexual acts). It is fortunate that writers are interested in psychoanalysis because, unlike analysts, they are free to think up thoughts unconstrained by the hypnotic effect of clinical practice. Good performers, like musicians or sportspeople or analysts, are often not that good at talking about what they do, partly because they are the ones who do it. There is nothing more limiting than actually doing something.

And the doing of it, like the living of any life, involves acknowledging, in one way or another, that there are only two sexes. In and of itself, this says nothing about the possible repertoire of gender identities. The logic of Judith Butler's argument, the kind of instructive incoherence she finds in Freud, recuperates a sense of possibility for analytic practice. And yet her lucidity also prompts another kind of reflection. It can sometimes seem a shame that there are only two sexes, not least because we then use this difference as a paradigm to do so much work for us (the differences between the sexes is, of course, more exciting, or more articulable, than the differences between a live body and a dead body). There is a kind of intellectual melancholy in this loss of a third sex that never existed and so can never be mourned; this third irrational sex that would break the spell (or the logic) of the two, and which is one of the child's formative and repressed fantasies about him- or herself (there is a link between this magical solution to the primal scene and fantasies of synthesis and redemption). What Freud called 'primary process' is, after all, the erasing of mutual exclusion, a logic defying logic. This form of generosity (and radicalism) is not always available, it seems, to our secondary-process selves.

III

More to the point & less composed.
Virginia Woolf, diary entry, 22 June 1940

Starting with two sexes, as we must – described as opposites or alternatives or complements – locks us into a logic, a limiting binary system, that often seems remote from lived, spoken experience, and is complicit with the other binary pairs – inside/outside, primary process/secondary process, sadism/masochism, patient/analyst, and so on – that are such a misleading part of psychoanalytic language. There is, as it were, always another alternative. We should be speaking of paradoxes and spectrums, not contradictions and mutual exclusion (and a world of paradox is a world without revenge: retaliation is a false cure for contradiction). 'The unconscious', Freud wrote in *The Claims of Psycho-Analysis to Scientific Interest*, 'speaks more than one dialect'. Voice is always in the plural. And the unconscious is a logic that dispels the illusion of minimal alternatives. Psychoanalysis, in other words, turns the idea of having it both ways upside down; it shows us that hypocrisy has been consistently underrated. We are never one thing or another, but a miscellany. (For how long in any given day is one homosexual or heterosexual, and can you always tell the difference?) Relationships constitute so-called identities, not the other way round, and this makes selves always provisional and circumstantial, not creatures of either/or (to suffer is often to feel a self fixed in something). Circumstances are always changing, whether we can allow ourselves to notice this or not. Defences are always defences against the provisional.

Every child and adolescent rightly wants to know whether there is a position beyond exclusion (or difference, or separateness, or identity), a world in which leaving and being left out disappears. This idea is taken up at a different level in Utopian socialism, which aims at a society without margins, and therefore without humiliation. These are not silly ideas, despite their marginalization in mainstream psychoanalysis, which can only maintain itself by fetishizing the idea of boundaries, by knowing best (the opposite of a fetish is an adventure). One of the contributions of British Middle Group psychoanalysis has been to prioritize the self as private property, and to describe both a pathology, and a necessity, of, its abolition (Milton and Winstanley are as much the precursors of Winnicott and Marion Milner, as are Freud and Melanie Klein).* This version of the self, inspired by fantasies of purity, becomes the enemy of free association; terrorized by exchange, its project is to define and sustain the idea of a real thing, to keep the self true. But the resolution of the Oedipus complex entails, among other things, the acknowledgement that there is no such thing as the real thing; the idea of the real thing is itself a fetish, complicit with all it excludes. It is the need for and belief in the real thing that is the problem for the Oedipal child.

It seems to be extremely difficult, in describing gender – or any of the so-called identities – to find a picture or a story that no longer needs the idea of exclusion. There seems to be something bewitching, certainly in psychoanalytic theory, about the idea – and the experience – of evacuation; and of the kinds of definition that the ideas of inside and outside can give us. (In relatively recent psychoanalytic history, Michael Balint was asking whether the fish was in the water or the water in the fish.) Why is it so difficult to imagine a life in which there is nothing to get rid of? In which men, for example, did not feel the need to dispose of their female selves? The self as expulsive is the self as exclusive. We are what we excrete.

*By the Middle Group here I am thinking specifically of the British psychoanalysts Winnicott, Khan, Milner, Rycroft and Laing. There is a buried connection between what might be called Christopher Hill's seventeenth century – the inspired Dissenters in the 1640s – and the Middle, or Independent, Group in British psychoanalysis.

The vocabulary of difference – the means of establishing those intra- and interpsychic boundaries and limits that psychoanalytic developmental theory promotes – is, by definition, far more extensive than the language of sameness (the same, of course, is not only the identical). We can talk about difference – in a sense, that's what talk is about, that's what language seems to be – but sameness appears to make us mute, dull or repetitive. To talk of homosexuality exclusively in terms that disparage sameness is to compound the muddle. Sameness, like difference, is a (motivated) fantasy not a natural fact – a construction, and, like all constructions, of its time, provisional. One of the reasons that we are currently addicted to difference is that difference makes competition possible; and competition is a cure for shame.

IV

Because I alone can perfectly forge my signature.
Jan Richman, 'Why I'm the Boss'

The language of boundaries that psychoanalysts, like estate agents, are so intent on, and that makes possible notions of identification and mourning, inevitably promotes a specific set of assumptions about what a person is and can be. It is a picture of a person informed by the languages of purity and property, by what Mary Douglas more exactly called purity and danger. It may be more useful to talk about gradations and blurring, to use a vocabulary of paradoχ, rather than contours and outlines when we plot our stories about gender. The language of performance – of continually making ourselves up, of trying out our parts – at least keeps definition on the move. After all, where else could it be?

'It is the difference in amount', Freud writes in *Beyond the Pleasure Principle*, 'between the pleasure of satisfaction which is demanded and that which is actually achieved that provides the driving factor which will permit of no halting at any position attained, but, in the poet's words, *ungebandigt immer vorwarts dringt* (presses ever forward unsubdued).' Satisfaction is hopeless. All the positions are unsatisfying because there is always another position. If, as Lacan insists, we are always in pursuit because we are in pursuit of something that isn't there, then it is also that gap, that inevitable disparity between desire and its object, that Freud alerts us to, that keeps us inventive and resilient, that gives us room for our selves. That gap is their stage. And sex is the act.

'Do not, above all', Nietzsche wrote in his preface to *Ecce Homo*, 'confound me with what I am not!' In Freud's view – nowhere more vividly confronted than in our sexuality – we are forever confounded with what we are not. (In psychoanalysis, paradoxically, a person is everything, both what he acknowledges and what he denies.) And, for that matter, though it is a blessing in disguise, we are forever unable to control people's interpretation of us. Psychoanalysis can show us how we try to control the interpretations, and how we are at risk when we succeed. There is a freedom – as well as a terror – in being able to be an object for others.

V

(Ah, this plethora of metaphors! I am like everything except myself.)

John Banville, *Athena*

Most psychoanalytic theory now is a contemporary version of the etiquette book; improving our internal manners, advising us on our best sexual behaviour (usually called maturity, or mental health, or a decentred self). It is, indeed, dismaying how quickly psychoanalysis has become the science of the sensible passions, as though the aim of psychoanalysis was to make people more intelligible to themselves rather than to realize how strange they are. When psychoanalysis makes too much sense, or makes sense of too much, it turns into exactly the symptom it is trying to cure: defensive knowingness. But there is nothing like sexuality, of course, for making a mockery of our self-knowledge. In our erotic lives, at least, our preferences do not always accord with our standards. We are excited by the oddest things, and sometimes people.

At its best, psychoanalysis usefully acknowledges the complexity of sexuality – that it is intrinsically conflictual, that pain and pleasure are versions of each other, that we don't know what we are talking about when we talk about sex. But it is surprisingly difficult to find in the psychoanalytic literature anything like a celebration of sexuality; or a sense that there really are states of sexual satisfaction, that sex can be ecstatic. From the abstraction of contemporary theory it can seem that people are more interested in having a sexual identity than in having a good time, more interested in the making or breaking of rules than in what the rules may be about. And psychoanalytic stories about the sexual revolution usually end up with a restoration of the monarchy. Freud's discovery of infantile sexuality and the radical changes in sexual mores since the 1960s produced, after all, only a brief flourish of sexual Utopianism in the inspired writings of Norman O. Brown and the rather more academic treatises of Herbert Marcuse (the concept of surplus repression could only have come out of a surplus of university teaching). Very quickly the masters of scarcity returned with their bracingly joyless languages of lack and absence: the 'truth' of the depressive position (Klein), and the necessity of the law of the father (Lacan); the need for 'firm boundaries', 'autonomous egos', and recognizable gender identities. From the psychoanalytic literature it was clear that thinking was better than stroking, and that people were in search of emotional maturity, self-knowledge or authenticity rather than passionate sex or affection. Spontaneity was the token virtue most psychoanalysts tended to affirm when writing about sexuality; but spontaneity is a delight only for conformists (as every child knows, it's the easiest thing in the world to learn). Sex, in fact, became a form of unhappiness; and so, as in all oppressive régimes, misery began to seem truthful. This is one of the sadder ironies of psychoanalysis, since Freud had showed us, perhaps better than anyone apart from Nietzsche, why self-punishing theories – ideologies of deprivation – are always morally prestigious. For some people, unhappiness is a moral obligation; and habit, Freud implied, was the modern word for duty. In our routines we are all ascetics.

The psychoanalytic relationship itself was the perfect picture for this new enlightened masochism: the patient pays the doctor not to touch him. Anyone, like Ferenczi or Reich, who questioned this was very quickly deemed, or actually became, mad (morally frightening and/or unintelligible). In a sense this ascetic imperative merely makes psychoanalysis similar to the great religions (a kind of Jewish Buddhism, say). And sustaining the Oedipal prohibition is, rightly, integral to the treatment. But there is an issue here that cannot be resolved either by huffy authoritarians or relaxed hedonists: from a psychoanalytic point of view, nobody can know about sexuality, no one is in a privileged position (because the parents *have* sex does not mean they know about it. What would it be to be an expert on sex, what would you know?). Laying down the law about sexuality either way is, so to speak, the line of least resistance. After all, what do we imagine sexuality is if it requires so much management? It is as though we have made the rules without knowing what the game is; as though the rules are there to stop us finding out.

If psychoanalysis gives us guide-lines about how to grow up sexually – developmental theory is a relief from our wayward unconsciousness, science as a cure for the demonic – it has also given us a language to question our sexual assumptions, and in particular our unconscious beliefs about the nature of, and possibilities for, satisfaction. (The question, Who decides what we can, or are able, to enjoy? joins psychoanalysis ineluctably to politics.) As the voice of glum realism, psychoanalysis has been perhaps a little too keen – suspiciously over-eager – to tell us persuasive stories about the necessities of frustration ('Everyone who practises renunciation', Adorno remarks, 'gives away more of his life than is given back to him'). Indeed Freud's notion of 'the wish to frustrate oneself' is nowhere more evident than in psychoanalytic writing about sexuality and identity, which is usually determinedly counter-erotic. When it comes to identity, now, more is better. When it comes to sexuality, though, more is a difficult word.

It is, of course, relatively recently that sexuality and identity have become inevitably twinned; the fact that we cannot imagine one without the other has become rather a mixed blessing. Either one, after all, is potentially a defence against – a refusal of – the other. If the demonic has been repressed in psychoanalytic theory – patholo-gized as the repetition compulsion, intense excitement becoming mania and perversion – it has also returned as the 'will to diagnosis'. Psychoanalytic writing is full of nicknames for people – borderline, psychotic, heterosexual, narcissistic, obsessional, etc. – that in some contexts can sound immensely authoritative (diagnosis has always been the way psychoanalysts tell themselves who they are). To generalize is to be a professional. But diagnosis is only part of a wider modern technology for identity acquisition. The risk – and this is nowhere more obvious than in the supposed need for a sexual identity – is that the wish to be defined is complicit with the wish to be controlled (or, more benignly, the wish to be looked after). Wanting to be defined by our sexuality may only be symptomatic of our wanting to be defined. But the unconscious, as Freud described it, always has a blurring effect (you thought you knew what you were saying and then, by making a slip or a pun, you say something else). In other words, psychoanalysis keeps in circulation what has become a useful cliché: that sexuality is what makes identity both necessary and impossible. Because we get lost in it, we want to know where we are.

The alternatives of being lost or being found are fundamental organizers of our experience; the Judaeo-Christian religions, like psychoanalysis itself, have always exploited the senses in which adults are similar to children (adults are more exploitable if you can convince them that they are really children, which is how seduction often works). But the language of being found – being recognizable, being the same as, having things in common, sharing – can obscure the pleasures of being lost. Not to mention the fact that speaking, implicitly or explicitly, in these quasi-religious terms about sexuality – in this language of redemption – coerces the conversation. In secular terms, being found means more or less fitting into one of the available categories. The risk is that we end up thinking that everyone is different but some are more different than others; or that being found means having just the right amount of sameness and difference. The question becomes: Do we want better generali-zations (more theory), or should we drop the whole project of trying to make them (read and write more novels and poems)? As every patient knows, and as every analyst should know, free-association is the death of theory. To talk about sex is always to talk about what we may or may not have in common; and this doubt about what we may or may not have in common is one of the things we have in common. Denial of difference is always a refusal of ignorance. Groups do not cohere against an external enemy; they cohere around collusive knowledge. It is conceivable that one of the things we use sexuality to do now is to talk about whether it is possible, or useful, or interesting, to make generalizations at all. Our categories should always be treated as questions – temporary groupings in which every element is nomadic – rather than as answers; as comforters but not as fetishes. Sexuality may be the modern cure for classification, rather than the other way round.

The paradox of sexuality, as it is constructed now, is that it both links us to other people, and makes us feel at odds with ourselves. That there can be no normal loving is potentially a liberating psychoanalytic idea; it makes room for more people and for more versions of more people. But it is still worth wondering what we think understanding sexuality will do for us, and what we think it is if it can be understood. (We might think: What else can we do but try to understand it?) If we banned the word love, it would be interesting to see what we found ourselves saying (and doing) to each other.

Because, from a psychoanalytic point of view, normality is a symptom, we have to be careful about what gets put in its place. Now that 'truth' has replaced sexual pleasure (in its broadest, Freudian sense) as *the* psychoanalytic ambition, normality is returning through the back door. No one can tell me that I'm not enjoying myself; they can only tell me that I shouldn't be. No one can tell me that I'm not telling the truth; they can only tell me that I should be. Without a passion for pleasure – without the unconscious – psychoanalysis becomes merely another glamorous or noble killjoy. In psychoanalysis one can see very clearly how two people can sit in a room together and try to kill each other's pleasure: the aim of analysis is to understand how this happens, and to restore their pleasure in each other's company.

Understanding sexuality – as if such a thing were possible – is just the beginning, if that. The difficult question is how we decide which kinds of loving are acceptable. Understanding does not inform our morality, our morality informs the ways we have of understanding. The language of pleasure and the language of justice are inextricable. By being a new way of saying this, psychoanalysis can be recruited either to consolidate our prejudices or to show us what our prejudices are for.

'Human beings', the philosopher Hilary Putnam writes, 'are self-surprising creatures.' If in our sexuality we are full of surprises, we are also, by the same token, keen to take the edge off our desire, eager to deaden ourselves. This is what Freud referred to as the battle between Eros and Thanatos, the hot war between aliveness and inertia. Freud showed us that there are surprises on both sides, but that it is the surprises that matter.

6
Minds

I

We seem never to ask, 'Why do you know?' or, 'How do you believe?'

J. L. Austin, *Other Minds*

One of the most famous, indeed constitutive, episodes in the story of the (Western) mind is the story Descartes tells of himself, as a character, sitting alone in a room and practising what he calls 'extensive doubt'. In his solitary quest for certainty – for that which he can reliably depend upon to be true, to be really there – 'the mind uses its own freedom and supposes the non-existence of all the things about whose existence it can have even the slightest doubt; and in so doing the mind notices that it is impossible that it should not itself exist during this time.' This project of ruthless doubt, this pursuit of the real, 'frees us from all our preconceived opinions . . . providing the easiest route by which the mind may be lead away from the senses'; we are led, Descartes writes, 'to recognize that the natures of the mind and body are not only different, but in some way opposite'. 'Opposite' meaning, here, in opposition to each other, but also, perhaps, suggesting that the body and the mind may be mutual saboteurs terrorizing each other. It is not exactly, Descartes implies, that we need to get away from the body, but that once we go in search of trustworthy foundations, of states of conviction, the body is the first casualty. As we shall see, the mind-object is that figure in the internal world that has to believe – and go on proving, usually by seeking accomplices – that there is no such thing as a body with needs. It is a fiction invented to solve the problem of wanting, to make the turbulence disappear. The body is misleading because it leads one into relationship, and so towards the perils and ecstacies of dependence and risk; it reminds us of the existence of other people. In this sense the mind-object – the mind imagined as an autonomous thing-person inside oneself – is a perverse theorist of the body.

Descartes, of course, was not the first person to think of the body as an object of suspicion, as the enemy of truth. Finding ways of not being bodies, the quest for something better, for an alternative to the body, to its desires and its death, is integral to both Platonism and Christianity. Truth, or redemption (the real), is what we are left with once we are free of the body (as though it is the sin or error of the body that it is finite, and therefore needs to be transcended: psychoanalysis brings transcendence down to earth). The need of the body and the death of the body make us think. For Winnicott, as we shall also see, it is a death, but a death at the beginning – a temporary and intimidating psychic death – that prompts the locating of an extreme version of what he calls a mind – a kind of internal expert. If, in early development, our 'bodily aliveness', our 'going-on-being', in Winnicott's words, is ruptured; if our existence is put under threat by an unmanageable environmental demand, we use our minds to maintain ourselves. Where there is a mind-object at work there is a loss, or a violation, or a terror, that cannot be acknowledged.

Descartes makes it very clear, though in a context of philosophical enquiry, that his very existence, his *belief* in his existence is under threat once he begins to doubt. Until, that is, he finds the thinking 'I'. 'Descartes establishes to his satisfaction', Stanley Cavell writes, 'that I exist only while, or *if and only if*, I think. It is this, it seems, which leads him to claim that the mind always thinks . . .'. For Descartes, thinking becomes the way people guarantee their existence (to themselves), establish their own presence in the world. My thoughts are inseparable from my sense of myself; indeed, they *are* my sense of myself, the only medium in which this sense can be. Like my home, they are where I live. For Descartes, in the *Meditations*, thought is the revelation that grounds him; his mind breaks his fall. 'At last', he writes in the Second Meditation,

I have discovered it – thought; this alone is inseparable from me. I am, I exist – that is certain. But for how long? For as long as I am thinking. For it could be that were I totally to cease from thinking, I should totally cease to exist. At present I am not admitting anything except what is necessarily true. I am, then, in the strict sense, only a thing that thinks; that is, I am a mind, or intelligence, or intellect, or reason – words whose meaning I have been ignorant of until now. But for all that I am a thing which is real and which truly exists. But what kind of thing? As I have just said – a thinking thing.

From a psychoanalytic point of view Descartes' discovery can be rediscovered. For example, is this not a precise formulation of some of the essential questions of childhood? What is inseparable from me, what is it I cannot bear to be separated from? And then, or therefore, what kind of thing am I? (And what kind of thing I am, or can be, depends upon that constitutive question of childhood, the litany of 'how long?') Faced with these fundamental questions, Descartes comes to rest in his mind, or rather, as a mind, a thinking thing. Mind, intelligence, intellect, reason – words born of necessity, insuring a future. As long as he thinks, he knows he is there, he knows where he is. But it is as though the mind is the only place left that he can be sure of being. One way of describing what he has discovered is that he is, in the telling phrase of the psychotherapists Corrigan and Gordon, sufficient unto his mind.

In terms of psychoanalysis Descartes' *Meditations* may seem both uncanny and germane. There are clearly overlapping preoccupations but there is also the instructive jarring (of vocabulary and allusion: I am using, for example, an English translation of Descartes' Latin text) that should remind us that we are in different worlds. If a straight line cannot be drawn from Descartes' *Meditations* to the psychoanalytic concept of the mind-object – and it cannot, because to do so would be to omit such an array of contexts – useful links can nevertheless be made (Descartes' use of the paradigm of dreaming and waking is something of a lure). There is, of course, no place in the Cartesian system for the unconscious; but how does one make a place for the unconscious? If, as Gerald Bruns has written, Descartes 'inaugurates a new era of epistemological thinking, wherein everything is thought to be determined or made intelligible by the workings of the mind', how is this different from Freud's psychoanalysis, or, indeed, from the concept of the mind-object? What stops psychoanalytic theory (and practice) from becoming a mind-object? How can you make a system, a psychic apparatus, that includes what cannot be known? Despite the existence of the unconscious, psychoanalysis always tends towards a covert Cartesianism. How can psychoanalysis keep the unknown in the picture? How can there be a theory of the unknown, a knowledge of the unknown, as psychoanalysis sometimes claims to be?

I want to read Winnicott's extraordinary paper, 'Mind and its Relation to the Psyche-Soma' (1949) as a critique – a pathologization – of Descartes' *Meditations* (it is characteristically Winnicottian in being a critique that makes no explicit reference to its object); and as a suspicion about psychoanalysis itself.

II

There is no meaning to the term intellectual health.
D. W. Winnicott, *Human Nature*

Winnicott begins his paper with a quotation from Ernest Jones that he has found quoted by Clifford Scott in his paper 'The Body Scheme in Psychotherapy'. 'I venture to predict', Jones wrote, 'that . . . the antithesis which has baffled all the philosophers will be found to be based on an illusion. In other words, *I do not think that the mind really exists as an entity* – possibly a startling thing for a psychologist to say' (Winnicott's emphasis). With this assertion, which Winnicott will go on to confirm, he uses Jones to refer indirectly to Descartes, among others ('all the philosophers . . .' seems rather blithe). If Winnicott had read the sentence before the one quoted by Scott, he would have found Jones in search, like Descartes, of foundations: describing psychoanalysis as a kind of Cartesian quest for essentials, Jones wrote, 'To ascertain what exactly comprises the irreducible mental elements, particularly those of a dynamic nature, constitutes, in my opinion, one of our most fascinating final aims.'

Where Descartes put the mind at the beginning of the story, Jones and Winnicott will put the body. But what kind of body? Replacing one term with another – dispelling the dualism of mind and body in the search for an origin, a true beginning – runs the risk of merely replacing one essentialism with another. The 'truth' of the body may be just another way of getting us to believe in the truth.

Endorsing Jones's assertion with one of his own – in the body scheme 'there is no obvious place for the mind' – Winnicott draws a distinction:

We are quite used to seeing the two words 'mental' and 'physical' opposed and would not quarrel with their being opposed in daily conversation. It is quite another matter, however, if the concepts are opposed in scientific discussion'.

Perhaps it is paradoxical, at the outset, that the mind is to be replaced by the body, but daily conversation is to be replaced by scientific discussion in the search for truth. From a scientific point of view, Winnicott writes, there is, 'the development of the individual from the very beginning of psycho-somatic existence'; there is a body composed of a psyche and a soma. We have to imagine the soma as the flesh-and-blood organism, a biological entity, and the psyche as 'the imaginative elaboration of somatic parts, feelings, and functions'. (It is not incidental, I think, that Winnicott does not define the word 'soma'.) If early development has been 'satisfactory', the 'mind does not exist as an entity in the individual's scheme of things'. It is, Winnicott writes, 'a false entity and a false localization'. The notion of a 'false entity', of course, begs a lot of questions. Good mind, Winnicott will go on to say, is the part of the self that will develop an understanding of its environmental deficits, in the service of a self-reliance that can sustain contact with, and need for, the mother. Bad mind – the 'false entity' that Corrigan and Gordon call the mind-object – is reactive to the trauma of environmental impingement, tries to abolish both the need and the object. With good-enough maternal care, in Winnicott's particular sense of these terms, the mind would be an ordinary participant in one's psychic life rather than an excessive preoccupation – a continuation of the mother one can take for granted, rather than a substitute which one is continually rigging up. So Descartes finding himself a 'thing that thinks' becomes, from Winnicott's point of view, symptomatic: a description of a developmental deficit. The mind, far from being a virtual definition, indeed a location of, the essentially human, becomes itself a distortion in the individual's psychosomatic development. Despite the special language – the albeit very different 'scientific discussion' – of Descartes and Winnicott, what is at stake here is what we believe a person, at his or her best, to be.

Descartes' narrator writes of himself as 'a thing which is real and which truly exists' only as 'a thinking thing'. Winnicott describes children who have had to exploit their minds for psychic survival, and of the consequent 'unrealness of everything to an individual who has developed in such a way'. In Winnicott's anti-Cartesian meditations, what he calls the mind is an attempted self-cure for a too-problematic dependence. Descartes depends on his mind to feel real. He is the 'I' that thinks. Descartes' solution is Winnicott's problem.

Of course, it is misleading, as I have said, to assume a continuity of vocabulary here; words like 'real', 'unreal', 'true', 'false', 'thinking', 'I' are born of histories and contexts (and translations). But it may be revealing to read Winnicott as wondering, in 'Mind and its Relation to the Psyche-Soma', What might have happened to someone – a contemporary – to make him ask the kinds of questions Descartes asks in his *Meditations*? What could lead you to doubt your own reality, to describe yourself, as Winnicott found some of his patients doing, as not feeling real? And how could one's very existence get bound up with what one knew (or remembered)? What is one relieved of, what is one managing, by certainty, by being an expert on oneself? Why does doubting start, and what is its terror (Winnicott refers in an early paper to 'the child's most sacred attribute: doubts about self')? And what kind of thing does each person assume a mind to be, and what kind of relationship can we have with it? Indeed, where do we get the idea of a mind as something – an object – with which we can have a relationship (lose it, feel mindless, say, 'Never mind', and so on)?

In Winnicott's view, the mind is that part of the self invented to cover for, to manage, any felt unreliability in the care-taking environment. It is a necessary fiction, born of expedience, and therefore potentially tainted by (unconscious) resentment. Whenever the world is not good enough, one has a mind instead. 'Here', Winnicott writes, echoing Descartes' opposition of mind and body,

in the overgrowth of the mental function reactive to erratic mothering, we see that there can develop an opposition between the mind and the psyche-soma, since in reaction to this abnormal environmental state the thinking of the individual begins to take over and organize the caring for the psyche-soma, whereas in health it is the function of the environment to do this. In health the mind does not usurp the environment's function, but makes possible an understanding and eventually a making use of its relative failure.

In the absence of a relatively reliable environmental provision, the mind becomes a kind of enraged bureaucrat, a master of circumstances. Winnicott describes the mind as 'cataloguing', exactly and completely, unmanageable – or rather, unimaginable – emotional experiences (in this sense the mind-object is the anti-type of the unconscious with its dream-work and its disregard for chronology). In states of privation thinking 'takes over', 'organizes', 'usurps'. It is not incidental that Winnicott's language hints at political insurrection. He is, after all, describing an internal psychic revolution. In 'health', one might say, using Winnicott's medical language, the mind listens to and collaborates with the body and its objects (or rather, subjects); in 'illness' there is a military coup and a dictator is installed called a mind-object, at once bureaucrat and terrorist. The mind knows that it does not know, and can use objects to find what it lacks; the mind-object cannot bear the kind of knowledge called not-knowing. The mind thrives on ignorance; the mind-object lives by convictions (and information: it is essentially an expert). From the point of view of the mind-object, at its most extreme, there can be no unconscious, because everything has already been accounted for ('a system', as Gerald Bruns writes in relation to Descartes, 'is almost by definition that which contains no secrets, because it allows nothing to be set apart'). But in a dictatorship, of course, everyone is under suspicion. As Corrigan and Gordon write, 'Patients who rely on their mind as an object, on some level, actually know all too well of its unreliability.' A baby cannot bring itself up.

What Winnicott, and Corrigan and Gordon after him, alerts us to with the concept of the mind-object, is the link between resourcelessness and the need to know. The mind, in Winnicott's account, is always making up for something, but something – sufficient maternal care – for which there is no substitute (any experience you need to know about, to understand, is a trauma). Knowing is the opposite of, the false self-cure for, dependence: 'acceptance of not knowing', Winnicott writes, 'produces tremendous relief . . .' In Bion's complementary language one could say: the mind-object attacks the link between the person and his desire, and the desire and its object. So Winnicott's concept of the mind confronts us with a paradox which has significant consequences for the practice of psychoanalysis: *we only need to know, be mindful of, that which we cannot trust depending on.*

The mind simulates reliability; knowing is a cure for the erratic (or the contingent). What, then, of the kind of knowing that goes on in, is prompted by, psychoanalysis?

III

All those attempts to bring everything in around you are part of
a naïve belief that you can recreate the whole world. Well, you
can't. Where would you put it? Next to the whole world?
David Hockney, 'On Photography'

When Winnicott refers to 'the overgrowth of the mental function reactive to erratic mothering', he gives us at least one description of the genesis of the mind-object. Erratic, though, is an interesting word. The *Shorter Oxford English Dictionary* offers these definitions: '1. Wandering; first used of the planets, and of certain diseases . . . 2. Vagrant, nomadic . . . 3. Having no fixed course . . . 4. Eccentric, irregular.' Even though clinically it is easy to understand what Winnicott means by erratic mothering, after Freud we might think of erratic as another word for the human – or, to put it another way, Is the unconscious an erratic mother? Certainly all the words in the dictionary definition would apply to Freud's description of the unconscious. Perhaps Winnicott in 'Mind and its Relation to the Psyche-Soma' is writing not only of an inter-psychic experience – between mother and child – but also about psychoanalysis itself? Is Winnicott's 'mind', for example, an unconscious parody, or caricature, of Freud's concept of the ego; and so is his paper a critique not only of erratic mothering but of psychoanalysis as a treatment in which the analyst strengthens the patient's mind? Or, to put it the other way around, is 'mother' also one of Winnicott's words for the unconscious? If, at best, a person should, as Winnicott says, 'live as a psyche-soma', what kind of relationship would a person have with their unconscious? What would a person's life be like if they lived as a psyche-soma, relatively mindless? Would the aim of a psychoanalysis be to know who you are, or to tolerate and enjoy the impossibility of such knowing? Winnicott's paper, I think, invites us to ask these kinds of questions.

Developmentally, Winnicott suggests, there was a time before the mind, when there was nothing to know about and no need to know. Once there is the trauma of impingement – once, as at birth, the environment becomes excessively demanding – the mind appears. But, as Winnicott implies, the mind is trying to know something that is not subject to knowing (like trying to look at something with one's mouth). The paradox here, which has difficult consequences for the notion of regression, is that the mental activity of the mind-object reinforces – secures, in a sense – the trauma it was trying to relieve; the mind that takes over sustains, by its very activity, the discontinuity of being that is the trauma. *The mind turns up when it is already too late.* If the environment had been as it should have been, the mind-object would have been unnecessary; its very existence signifies insult and betrayal (this is the root of hatred of the mind, of its very existence; for some children and adolescents, failing at school is the only alternative to psychosomatic illness as a self-cure. To sabotage the mind becomes a way of returning to the body). In the light of Winnicott's developmental picture, it would make sense that in psychoanalysis one might aim to reconstruct the cumulative trauma that made the mind-object necessary as a solution, but also to enable the patient to have access to that time before the mind. Does psychoanalysis, therefore, sponsor a more benign mind-object – one that is capable of using insight about the genesis of its mind-object – or does it aim to facilitate its absence, or both? Is psychoanalysis a way of teaching people how to get lost again (in thought)? Winnicott's concept of the mind raises the constitutive psychoanalytic question of the relationship between regression – even the ordinary regression of free-association – and so-called insight. Where in Winnicottian analysis does the mind come in? To this Winnicott's paper seems to reply: *the mind always comes in afterwards* (to repair, to reflect, to reconstruct, to formulate, to consider, to fetishize, etc.). All thoughts are afterthoughts. It is as though the project of the mind is essentially damage limitation. Why is it so difficult to imagine an analysis that consists exclusively of free-association?

But because the mind always comes in afterwards – after the trauma, after the state of absorption or free-association – it always runs the risk of being a pre-emptive presence. The mind-object has always unconsciously identified with the traumatic agent (or rather, events) that first prompted its existence; its function then becomes, to impinge, to interrupt, to punctuate. The mind that attempted to repair – to compensate for – the trauma becomes the trauma itself. The mind, in other words, becomes the patient's cumulative – in fact, accumulating – trauma. A trauma that the analyst might feel some solidarity with.

IV

My intellect, or whatever one usually works with, is also on vacation.

Freud to Ferenczi, 4 August 1911

It was Ferenczi who first suggested that the patient is not cured by free-associating, he is cured *when he can free-associate*. I think it was

Ferenczi's sense that psychoanalysis was potentially a form of mind-object – a facilitating of the mind-object – that in part led him towards his particular kind of courageous clinical experiments. His formative paper 'Confusion of Tongues between the Adults and the Child' (1933) – an unacknowledged precursor of Winnicott's paper – is about the kind of trauma that makes a child knowing (and the kind of trauma that can turn someone into a psychoanalyst). Psychoanalysis as a quest for reliable knowledge about the self (and the object) is a covert continuation of the Cartesian project; psychoanalysis as the facilitation of the (psychic) time before the mind – call it the capacity to free-associate, the capacity to be absorbed – is a very different project. Both, of course, have their uses, their necessary occasions.

Psychoanalysis was born, in a sense, of the relationship inside Freud between the Cartesian and the anti-Cartesian, the psychoanalyst and the dreamer. Both Ferenczi and Winnicott were struggling, I think, with the Cartesian in Freud and in psychoanalysis itself: what Gerald Bruns calls 'the Cartesian collapse of being into the logically possible'. And the logically possible becomes that which can be known. A psychoanalysis committed to the 'logically possible' seems like a contradiction in terms. In different ways Winnicott and Ferenczi confronted this irony by proposing experience – a certain kind of emotional experience – as an alternative to insight (or self-knowledge) as the legitimate aim of psychoanalysis. It is not incidental that Ferenczi, and his student Balint, and Winnicott, and his students Khan and Milner, were pioneers of the idea of regression in psychoanalytic treatment. The word regression is a way of referring to those states of mind (or mindlessness), either inarticulate or on the verges of representation, that defy or confound the already known. A regression is a revision, what Winnicott calls a surprise. The opposite of regression is not progress but omniscience (there is nothing more time-consuming than omniscience). It entails the risk of entrusting oneself – something we do every day, without thinking, when we are momentarily lost in thought. Or in the kind of psychoanalysis in which we can forget ourselves. The idea of knowing oneself makes a fetish out of memory.

In the absence of trauma, Winnicott implies – as if there could be such a thing – there is nothing worth knowing. The concept of the mind-object reminds us that we know things at our own cost; and that knowing is not the only thing we can do. Psychoanalysis can add to the story of the mind, the story of the mind on vacation.

Freud's account of obsessional neurosis – a foreboding of what psychoanalysis itself might become – is a critique of knowledge as privilege, and of the privileging of knowledge. The obsessional exposes the violence, the narrow-mindedness, of a certain kind of expertise about the self. If psychoanalysis doesn't also facilitate the patients' capacity not to know themselves, it becomes merely another way of setting limits to the self; and the analyst becomes an expert on human possibility, something no one could ever be, despite the posturing of our own favourite authorities. There are always too many good reasons to be impressed by impossibility. At its best, psychoanalysis can show us both what we have in mind, and what we mind about, and the relationship, if any, between them. But it cannot tell us who we can be. It can tell us, though, that prescription begins when curiosity breaks down. Too much definition leaves too much out.

Bibliography

Theodor Adorno and Max Horkheimer, *Dialectic of Enlightenment* (London, Verso, 1979)

Didier Anzieu, *The Skin Ego* (New Haven, Yale University Press, 1989)

Michael Balint, *The Basic Fault* (London, Tavistock Publications, 1968)

Leo Bersani, *The Freudian Body* (New York, Columbia University Press, 1986)

– *The Culture of Redemption* (Cambridge, Harvard University Press, 1990)

– *Homos* (Cambridge, Harvard University Press, 1995)

R. P. Blackmur, *Language as Gesture* (London, Allen and Unwin, 1954)

Gerald L. Bruns, *Inventions* (New Haven, Yale University Press, 1982)

Mikkel Borch-Jacobsen, *The Freudian Subject* (London, Macmillan, 1989)

– *The Emotional Tie* (Stanford, Stanford University Press, 1993)

Judith Butler, *Gender Trouble* (London, Routledge, 1992)

– 'Melancholy Gender/Refused Identification' in *Psychoanalytic Dialogues*, Vol. 5, No. 1, 1995

John Cage, *M* (Middletown, CT, Wesleyan University Press, 1973)

Stanley Cavell, *In Quest of the Ordinary* (Chicago, Chicago University Press, 1988)

Nina Coltart, *Slouching Towards Bethlehem* (London, Free Association Books, 1992)

Corrigan and Gordon, eds., *The Mind-Object* (New Jersey, Aronson, 1995)

René Descartes, *Meditations on First Philosophy*, trans. John Cottingham (Cambridge, Cambridge University Press, 1986)

Mary Douglas, *Purity and Danger* (London, Routledge Kegan and Paul, 1969)

Mark Edmundson, *Literature against Philosophy* (Cambridge, CUP, 1995)

Sándor Ferenczi, *First Contributions to Psychoanalysis* (London, Hogarth Press, 1952)

– *Final Contributions to the Problems and Methods of Psychoanalysis* (London, Hogarth Press, 1955)

– *The Clinical Diary of Sándor Ferenczi*, ed. J. Dupont (Cambridge, Harvard University Press, 1988)

Sigmund Freud, *The Standard Edition of the Complete Psychological Works of Sigmund Freud*, ed. and trans. James Strachey (London, Hogarth Press, 1953–74)

– *Letters of Sigmund Freud, 1873–1939* ed. Ernst L. Freud (Hogarth Press, 1960)

Sigmund Freud and Sándor Ferenczi, *The Correspondence*, Vol. 1, ed. Eva Brabant, Ernst Falzeder, Patrizia Giampieri-Deutsch (Cambridge, Harvard University Press, 1993)

Ernest Gellner, *Reason and Culture* (Oxford, Blackwell, 1994)

Jean-Joseph Goux, *Oedipus, Philosopher*, trans. Catherine Porter (Stanford, Stanford University Press, 1993)

Christopher Hill, *The World Turned Upside Down* (London, Penguin, 1975)

– *The Experience of Defeat* (London, Faber, 1984)

Edmond Jabès, *A Foreigner Carrying in the Crook of his Arm a Tiny Book*, trans. Rosemary Waldrop (Hanover, Wesleyan University Press, 1993)

Ernest Jones, 'A Valedictory Address', *International Journal of Psychoanalysis*, XXVII, 1946, pp. 11–12

– *Papers on Psychoanalysis* (London, Hogarth Press, 1948)

– Sigmund Freud, *Life and Work* (London, Hogarth Press, 1953)

Franz Kafka, *Parables and Paradoxes* (New York, Schocken, 1961)

M. Masud R. Khan, *The Privacy of the Self* (London, Hogarth Press, 1974)

Jacques Lacan, *Ecrits* (London, Tavistock, 1977)

– *The Four Fundamental Concepts of Psychoanalysis* (London, Hogarth Press, 1977)

Frank Lentricchia, *Modernist Quartet* (Cambridge, CUP, 1994)

Jane Miller, *Working Time* (Ann Arbor, University of Michigan Press, 1992)

Marion Milner, *The Suppressed Madness of Sane Men* (London, Tavistock, 1987)

Friedrich Nietzsche, *Ecce Homo*, trans. R. J. Hollingdale (London, Penguin, 1979)

J. B. Pontalis, *Frontiers in Psychoanalysis* (London, Hogarth Press, 1981)

Hilary Putnam, *Pragmatism* (Oxford, Blackwell, 1995)

John Rickman, *Selected Contributions to Psychoanalysis* (London, Hogarth Press, 1957)

Jean-Paul Sartre, *The Transcendence of the Ego*, trans. Forrest Williams and Robert Kirkpatrick (New York, Farrar, Straus and Giroux, 1975)

Frederick Seidel, *My Tokyo* (New York, Farrar, Straus and Giroux, 1993)

Idries Shah, *The Exploits of the Incomparable Mulla Nasrudin* (London, Pan, 1973)

– *The Pleasantries of the Incredible Mulla Nasrudin* (London, Pan, 1975)

Quentin Skinner, 'Moral Ambiguity and the Renaissance Art of Eloquence', *Essays in Criticism*, Vol. XLIV, No. 4, October 1994

Paul Valéry, quoted in Stephen Dunn, *Walking Light* (New York, Norton, 1993)

D. W. Winnicott, *The Child, The Family and the Outside World* (London, Penguin, 1964)

– *Through Paediatrics to Psychoanalysis* (London, Hogarth Press, 1975)

– *Human Nature* (London, Free Association Books, 1988)

Ludwig Wittgenstein, *On Certainty* (Oxford, Blackwell, 1968)

– *Philosophical Investigations* (Oxford, Blackwell, 1953)

William Wordsworth, *The Prelude*, ed. J. C. Maxwell (London, Penguin, 1972)

Index